JESUS:
The Main Thing
FROM GENESIS TO REVELATION

Michael J Gibbs

Copyright © 2014 Authored By Michael J Gibbs
All rights reserved.

ISBN: 0615988792
ISBN 13: 9780615988795
Library of Congress Control Number: 2014905086
LCCN Imprint Name: Michael Gibbs, Colorado Springs, CO

TABLE OF CONTENTS

PREFACE

My wife has always said that I am a bottom line person. Beating around the bush doesn't work very well for me. So, right off the bat I would like to address why I have expended the effort to write this book. I believe that the Christian world today has broadly become more attentive to defending denominational and/or individual belief systems than focusing on the personal love relationship with Jesus Christ that Scripture clearly teaches is the "main thing" God is seeking from those who would call Him Lord. The Bible is clear that God wants His people (church) to be united (one with Him and one another) in Him, not fussing and fighting over whose viewpoint is the one that brings about the heavenly life. In general, I believe much of the church of today is in the same position as the church at Ephesus was in Revelation 2. In the beginning they were abiding in the love of Christ that flows from the heart of God into the heart of His people. Jesus tells them that by drifting into external religious dogma, they had unwittingly distanced themselves from Him personally and if they did not repent and return to Him, it was going to cost them their lampstand (No, I don't know for sure what that means but I think it involves serious loss). I really believe He is speaking that same Word to us today. "Come back to Me. I love you and I want your love, not your dutiful, religious service". I am convinced that when Christians will center their spiritual attention directly on the "one true doctrine" (the Gospel) that Jesus the Christ is to be the focal point of our affection, the church will experience the unity and power we are supposed to be executing in His name. This book is written from the point of view that Jesus has always been the "Main Thing" from Genesis to Revelation. When Scripture is examined from that singular interpretative perspective light will shine truth on many of the long held, man created belief systems that are so prevalent in the church today.

I did not set out in the beginning to write a book. It started for me several years ago when a few people whom I had known from ministry circles we traveled in joined with groups that believed in and focused much of their attention on attempting to follow Old Testament laws and ordinances. They explained that this was the will of God for Christian's who wanted to hear Jesus say "well done, faithful servant" when He returns finding them working to remove their "spots and wrinkles". They advise that a wise Christian will have a desire "to get back in touch with his Jewish roots". At that time I could not explain the reasons for why I was so resistive in my spirit to this teaching. My first inclination was that something must be wrong with me because most of these people were sincere profess-ing Christians, some we had served with in church and on mission trips. The degree of my concern was considerably upsetting and motivated me to start researching deeply into what truth I could locate concerning the links between Jesus Christ and Old Testament reality. This led to a maze of "theological" information that was anything but easy to process. I real-ized quickly that my knowledge and understanding of how the Old and New Testaments work together was sorely lacking.

I definitely needed a much greater comprehension of who Jesus Christ is, was and is to be. I had never given much thought to there being a "central-ity" of the Gospel message in both the Old and New Testaments. As I began to comprehend more about the purpose of Christ's mission as fore-told in the Old Testament, I began to understand more about the Bible (in entirety) and the heart intent of God toward His beloved creation. What I discovered on this journey has forever changed my life. It also provided answers for why I experienced the resistance to the "Jewish roots" activity.

During this process, I put my findings in writing. Eventually, I felt led to put the information in book form. Some of the questions addressed in this work are as follows:

1. Does the Bible have one central message or is it a complex mixture of allegory and moral guidelines designed to be open to many interpretations?

2. To whom were the promises of Abraham made?

3. Do the Old and New Testaments flow together in continuity or do they serve separate purposes?

4. Does God have two groups of "chosen people" or one?

5. Is there a difference between "ethnic Israel" and "spiritual Israel" or are they one and the same.

6. Does God have a different plan for Jewish people who reject the gift of Jesus Christ than for everyone else?

7. What is the purpose and significance of "God's Law"?

8. Can we identify who is really the "true Israel of God?

9. What is the distinction between God the Father and Jesus the Christ?

10. Does God have a heart and if so, what is in it?

At this early stage, one might legitimately ask what some of these issues have to do with Jesus Christ, "The Main Thing". I can only affirm that they do. If you stay with me, chapter after chapter considers Jesus, from Genesis to Revelation, and will ultimately lead to what Scripture has to say about "all of the above" and how they relate to the importance of finding that "secret place" of abiding "in Christ". I repeat that I believe that much of the church today has been inadvertently distanced from the original intent of God's heart concerning the plan of redemption in Christ that He put in place before the foundation of the world. Only by focusing our spiritual searching back on increasing our intimacy with the person of Jesus Christ can we assure that the Gospel will remain pure and undistorted.

My prayer is that the information in this writing will be of some value to those of us who have a desire to see Jesus occupying the position where He belongs, first place in our lives.

INTRODUCTION

※

"Those who impartially search after truth will come to the knowledge of it"
(Matthew Henry) [1]

While in pursuit of truth from the Word of God, I began to see things in Scripture that I could not get to match up and make sense with much of what I had been taught and just accepted as truth over most of my Christian life. I found that there is no "duplicity" in Christ Jesus. He and He alone is the "single message" Gospel from Genesis to Revelation. A lot of the issues I was confused about in some way involve how that solitary Gospel message of "the Christ" interfaces with the ancient and current day nation of Israel and Jewish people. I mention that upfront because I think there is much misconception today over the relationship of true Christianity to Old Testament Israel and whether or not God has two separate "chosen peoples". While the central purpose of this work is to magnify Jesus Christ and not to debate controversial issues, I find that discussion regarding the connection between the Church of Jesus Christ and Old Testament Israel is unavoidable. My reasoning is that if God indeed has two separate groups of "chosen people" so be it. If, in actuality He only has one, then lending support and referring to the wrong group as "God's chosen" could be denigrating to the other. I understand that this will step on a lot of toes. It stepped on mine in a big way.

I am not a highly educated scholar but one who has been searching the Scriptures daily for years. I have a personal relationship with Jesus and as that relationship has grown (still growing daily) I have had to accept that many aspects of doctrines pertaining to Israel and the Jewish people I had previously held were not compatible with what I was gleaning from the Word. Looking back, I can say with candor that I had never bothered to study the Bible from a "Main Thing" or "singular theme" perspective that I now follow. For me, the controversy is settled in my heart today because of the truths that I have discovered seeking the Scripture from a "Jesus is everything" point of reference.

I have attempted to assemble and present Scripture in sequences that make difficult passages easier for me to understand regarding what I believe to be the sum and substance of all truth, namely Jesus Christ Himself.

Christians are expected to study the Word of God in pursuit of truth. Possession of the truth leads us into intimate relationship with God Himself. We are advised to seek with our "whole heart". Apparently anything less than whole hearted will not work too well because we have an enemy of our soul who would like to steal the truth from us and keep us from reaching the full "knowledge" of God. The Word says this enemy is the ruler of the world system we live in and that he is only able to have influence on us by getting us to believe things that are not true. His only power is deception. He uses half-truth and spins it to make it appear to be reality. He has absolutely no power over us when we know and comprehend the truth. The Bible calls this enemy satan. Who is this satan:

"People's beliefs concerning Satan range from the silly to the abstract—from a little red guy with horns who sits on your shoulder urging you to sin, to an expression used to describe the personification of evil. The Bible, however, gives us a clear portrait of who Satan is and how he affects our lives. Put simply, the Bible defines Satan as an angelic being who fell from his position in heaven due to sin and is now completely opposed to God, doing all in his power to thwart God's purposes.

Satan was created as a holy angel. Isaiah 14:12 possibly gives Satan's pre-fall name as Lucifer. Ezekiel 28:12-14 describes Satan as having been created a cherubim, apparently the highest created angel. He became arrogant in his beauty and status and decided he wanted to sit on a throne above that of God (Isaiah 14:13-14; Ezekiel 28:15; 1 Timothy 3:6). Satan's pride led to his fall. Notice the many "I will" statements in Isaiah 14:12-15. Because of his sin, God barred Satan from heaven.

Satan became the ruler of this world and the prince of the power of the air (John 12:31; 2 Corinthians 4:4; Ephesians 2:2). He is an accuser (Revelation 12:10), a tempter (Matthew 4:3; 1 Thessalonians 3:5), and a deceiver (Genesis 3; 2 Corinthians 4:4; Revelation 20:3). His very name means "adversary" or "one who opposes." Another of his titles, the devil, means "slanderer."

Even though he was cast out of heaven, he still seeks to elevate his throne above God. He counterfeits all that God does, hoping to gain the worship of the world and encourage opposition to God's kingdom. Satan is the ultimate source behind every false cult and world religion. Satan will do anything and everything in his power to oppose God and those who follow God. However, Satan's destiny is sealed—an eternity in the lake of fire" (Revelation 20:10). 2

Within the last few years I happened upon what I believe to be the "fundamental key" that cuts through satan's deception, leads directly to absolute truth and exposes the devil's counterfeiting lies. I am writing to share that perspective with "whosoever will" have interest. Allow me to explain further:

I am an impartial seeker of truth and a Christian since 1958. Though raised a Christian, I could not have been considered much of a Bible student at all until around 1990. Until then, I had just accepted that the denominational doctrines I was exposed to growing up were totally true, and besides, it didn't really matter all that much because, in reality, my faith at that time was much lower in priority to "more important" material life pursuits. It was about that time that one of a series of life changing events shook me spiritually and motivated me to want to learn more about God. The Bible says that knowledge of God comes "precept upon precept, precept upon precept, line upon line, line upon line, here a little, there a little" (Is.28:10). In other words, discovering Biblical truth is a progressive process. As my knowledge of God began to gradually increase, truth became much more difficult to conclude. In the Christian community, so many opinions, interpretations and doctrines of what God has said to us in His Word, all supposedly undergirded by the Gospel of Jesus Christ. When one doesn't know what he doesn't know, he often tends to rest on the credence of those he thinks know more than he does. As belief patterns are formed around traditions and teaching of men, the tendency is oftentimes to defend "what I have always just believed" rather than to search deeper into the Scriptures. I think Christians do this a lot without realizing it; likely most all of us at one time or another to some degree. Over the years man has come up with countless versions of God's message to His people sent to us in the Bible, His Holy Word. If one Googles "10,000 religions and 34,000 denominations" he will find information from an organization that has identified over 10,000 different religions in the world, all claiming to have connection with a god or a way of life. More astonishingly, they say there are approximately 34,000 denominations within Christianity, all having distinctions that set them apart from the others. Think about that for a moment; 34,000 versions of one straightforward truth. How can that be? One of the last prayers of Jesus while on earth was that His people (Christians) would be <u>one</u> as He and the Father are One. (John 17:11, 22, 23). Denominations tend to divide rather than unite, don't they? The people of God are supposed to function as one Body. In my experience and observation, unity is the exception rather than the rule. What if we functioned in "one accord" like the early church? I saw a statistic the other day that pointed out that if all professing Christians would contribute just .25 cents per week to a unified fund, it could be enough to mostly eliminate world hunger.

Scripture is clear that God's will for His people is unity and not division. I believe that if we would focus more intently on the "one true Gospel" (what

I refer to continually as "the Main Thing") instead of our denominational traditions we would find it much easier to walk together in agreement.

> *But I urge and entreat you, brethren, by the name of our Lord Jesus Christ,*
> *that all of you be in perfect harmony and full agreement in what you say,*
> *and that there be no dissensions or factions or divisions among you, but*
> *that you be perfectly united in your common understanding and in your*
> *opinions and judgments. (1 Cor.1:10 AMP)*

Where do all these different versions come from? Scripture tells us we have the Holy Spirit to lead us into all truth, but as previously noted, we have that adversary spirit busily at work scheming to lead us away from the true, saving knowledge of God and His Christ and divide us against ourselves.

> *[1]Boys (lads), it is the last time (hour, the end of this age). And as you have heard that*
> *the antichrist [he who will oppose Christ in the guise of Christ] is coming, even now*
> *many antichrists have arisen, which confirms our belief that it is the final (the end) time.*
> *(1 John 2:18 AMP)*

This passage clearly conveys that we have been in the last days for quite a while and that there are spirits at work that can masquerade to appear Christ like but in fact are His enemies. The Apostle Paul warns of them to the Corinthians:

> *These people are false apostles. They are deceitful workers who disguise*
> *themselves as apostles of Christ. But I am not surprised! Even Satan*
> *disguises himself as an angel of light. So it is no wonder that his servants also*
> *disguise themselves as servants of righteousness. In the end they will get the*
> *punishment their wicked deeds deserve.*
> *(2 Cor. 11:13-15 NLT)*

We reemphasize that the Holy Spirit, the Spirit of all truth has an adversary that counterfeits the Word of God. As the people of God, it is our obligation to discern the difference.

Dear friends, do not believe every spirit, but test the spirits to see whether they are from God, because many false prophets have gone out into the world. This is how you can recognize the Spirit of God: Every spirit that acknowledges that Jesus Christ has come in the flesh is from God, but every spirit that does not acknowledge Jesus is not from God. This is <u>the spirit of the antichrist</u>, which you have heard is coming and even now is already in the world.
(1 John 4:1-3 NIV)

We have just heard straight from the Word of God that Christians have a rival that is so deceptive that he is able to make us believe we are following after God when we are often unwittingly falling prey to his lying schematics. His tactics are described as "anti-christ" (against Christ; the anointed One). Please notice the term is anti <u>Christ</u> and not anti <u>God</u> or anti <u>Jesus.</u> The full force of his purpose is to get us to believe something false pertaining to Jesus, <u>The Christ</u>. The spirit of antichrist has the ability to appear to be the right and true way but in fact is the mirror opposite. This spirit of antichrist is much more subtle and devious than most Christians ever acknowledge. One testament to that fact is the 34,000 different versions of "the one true Gospel" that is not supposed to be divided, with each faction believing his edition is the truth.

To those who say that any mention of the devil and the power of his deception is giving place to him instead of concentrating on the power of God, my response is always the same. The quickest way to be defeated by an inferior foe is to underestimate or disregard his capabilities. As a Vietnam infantry veteran, I am qualified to attest first hand to the veracity of that statement.

The negative, evil force (satan) has been around a long time. Way back in the beginning (Gen. 4:7) God tells Cain that the spirit of sin is "lying at the door" to destroy him. He (God) makes it clear that Cain has the ability and is expected to rule over this spirit.

This describes our daily battle fairly well, doesn't it? How do we guard against being deceived into missing the mark? How do we defeat the counterfeit messages of the evil one? Is there a good way? Is there a best way? I believe there is.

While plugging away searching for answers to my questions (trying to get it right), I discovered a "fundamental" key to understanding Scripture that has profoundly deepened my comprehension of the Word of God and has empowered me with significantly greater ability to discern between truth and falsehood. I am still amazed (and embarrassed) that it has taken me 50+ years of Christian life and ministry to come to this simple, eye open-ing reality, "the greater our knowledge of the authentic, the less likely we will fall for the imitation". The message is not complex. It is remarkably and marvelously straightforward. However, simple does not always mean easy. I can say with conviction that this step forward has been the most important, life-changing occurrence, among many before in my 55 years of Christian experience.

I am writing to share that key with "whosoever will" find it beneficial. I have attempted to present Scripture in a manner that demands answers and reckoning as opposed to issuing a "challenge to popular Scriptural interpretative methodology". I am not naïve to the fact that there will be those who will view it as controversial, but I remain hopeful that "impar-tial seekers of truth" who have not yet happened upon this "key" realiza-tion will find it especially worthwhile.

God Bless

Michael J Gibbs

The Main Thing

THE KEY

———⊗⊗⊗———

Have you ever seen the quote "the main thing is to keep the main thing the main thing"? Clear and simple, that is the fundamental key that I will be forever grateful that I have learned.

The Bible repeatedly proclaims to be God's Word. Does God's Word have a "main thing" or is it merely a book of allegory, figurative and symbolic stories that promote ethical and moral values for men to build sermons from? When God sent His Communication to mankind through inspired men in the Bible, was there a "main thing" He desired for us to grasp or did He want us to vacillate among the 30+ thousand different versions so we would stay confused? God is not the author of confusion (1 Cor. 14:33). Proverbs 4 tells us to get wisdom and understanding (knowledge of God) at all cost. 1Timothy 2:4 says "God our Savior desires all men to be saved and to come to the knowledge of the truth". What does that mean? Are there numerous "main things" for us to discover as we separate the Old and New Testaments in our personal and corporate "Bible studies"? Or is there one central message, one "main" thematic that remains consistent from Genesis to Revelation that makes all the "puzzling" pieces fit together to present one beautiful, big picture?

Read this excerpt from the book of Hosea and see if you think it contains a clue:

*"The Lord says, "Israel, what should I do with you? Judah, what should I
do with you? Your faithfulness is like a morning mist, like the dew that goes
away early in the day. I have warned you by my prophets
that I will kill you and destroy you. My justice comes out like bright light.
I want faithful love more than I want animal sacrifices. I want people to
know me more than I want burnt offerings." (Hosea 6:4-6 NCV)*

The main theme of the Bible is God's desire for love and relationship. It
was broken with Adam. It was restored through Christ. When we accept
the gift of Christ and fix our love and devotion on Him, we are reconciled
back into that love. Knowing God and His love through a personal relationship with The Son, Jesus Christ is the "Main Thing" in all of Scripture!

That's how it began and that's how God wants it to end for His people.
Throughout the Bible, God shares story after story of the prophecy of his
Son, the hope of repentance, and asks us for our true love for Him.

Consider the following Scripture:

"Teacher, which command in the law is the most important?"

*Jesus answered, "'Love the Lord your God with all your heart, all your soul,
and all your mind. This is the first and most important command. ³⁹ And
the second command is like the first: 'Love your neighbor as you love
yourself.'* **All** *the law and the writings of the prophets depend on these two
commands." (Matt. 22:36-40 NCV)*

God IS love. He wants us to love Him and each other. This is God's law. How
can one love God if he does not know Him? I was well along in my Christian
life before I realized that the essence of eternal life is "knowing God".

*And this is the way to have eternal life—to know you, the only true God,
and Jesus Christ, the one you sent to earth.(John 17:3 NLT)*

Many people think knowing a lot of Scripture and attending church and being heavily involved in spiritual activities translates to eternal life. The Word says be careful about believing that.

You search and investigate and pore over the Scriptures diligently, because you suppose and trust that you have eternal life through them. And these [very Scriptures] testify about Me! And still you are not willing [but refuse] to come to Me, so that you might have life. (John 5:39-40 AMP)

The Scriptures are alive with Christ and their purpose is to bring us to the knowledge of Him, but the life is in "knowing Him" personally and intimately. Hear what the Apostle Paul says about this:

Yes, everything else is worthless when compared with the infinite value of knowing Christ Jesus my Lord. For his sake I have discarded everything else, counting it all as garbage, so that I could gain Christ and become one with him. I no longer count on my own righteousness through obeying the law; rather, I become righteous through faith in Christ! For God's way of making us right with himself depends on faith. I want to know Christ and experience the mighty power that raised him from the dead. I want to suffer with him, sharing in his death, (Phil.3:8-10 NLT)

This is really clear. Paul says NOTHING compares with "knowing" Christ. I believe he is suggesting that we experience the "mighty power that raised Christ from the dead" in our lives as it flows routinely out of true relationship (knowing Him), not just knowing about Him. There are many passages that tell us the same thing but one I like the best is found in Psalm 91. This is a powerful chapter of God's Word that lays out precious promises for those who know and trust God and abide in His "secret place". What He reveals in verses 14-16 say an enormous amount about the importance of knowing Him:

*Because he has set his love upon Me, therefore will I deliver him; I will set
him on high, <u>because he knows and understands My name [has a personal
knowledge</u> of My mercy, love, and kindness—trusts and relies on Me,
knowing I will never forsake him, no, never]. He shall call upon Me, and
I will answer him; I will be with him in trouble, I will deliver him and
honor him. With long life will I satisfy him and show him My salvation
(Psalm 91:14-16 AMP)*

All of these affirming promises and assurances belong to those who know
God personally and are abiding in His love ("dwelling in that secret place
of The Most High").

Two of the most disturbing passages of Scripture in the Bible are where
Jesus clearly warns that there will be many who think they are ready to
meet Him because of things they have done in His name, only to be
rebuked by Him at his second coming because they did not bother to get
to "know Him".

*"Not everyone who calls out to me, 'Lord! Lord!' will enter the Kingdom
of Heaven. Only those who actually do the will of my Father in heaven will
enter ² On judgment day <u>many</u> will say to me, 'Lord! Lord! We prophesied in
your name and cast out demons in your name and performed many miracles
in your name.' ²³ But I will reply, '<u>I never knew you.</u> Get away from me, you
who break God's laws.' (Matt. 7:21-23 NLT)*

The same exact message is repeated in the parable of the ten virgins.

*Later, when the other five bridesmaids returned, they stood outside, calling,
'Lord! Lord! Open the door for us!' "But he called back, 'Believe me, <u>I
don't know you!</u>' (Matt. 25:11-12 NLT)*

Please don't miss the fact that all ten virgins thought they were going
out to meet the bridegroom. Half of them had somehow not ever been
acquainted with Him even though they must have thought otherwise!

On that day, (and it literally could be any day now) MANY who call Him Lord are going to receive the shock wave of their life when they discover that they missed the "Main Thing". What a tragic, eternal, uncorrectable (at that time) mistake.

And the Word (Christ) became flesh (human, incarnate) and tabernacled (fixed His tent of flesh, lived awhile) among us; and we [actually] saw His glory (His honor, His majesty), such glory as an only begotten son receives from his father, full of grace (favor, loving-kindness) and truth.
(John 1:14 AMP)

The "Main Thing", Immanuel (God Himself with us) became flesh (Jesus Christ) and lived among us in a human body for the purpose of reconciling us back to God (Himself). He loved us that much, to live a sinless life that qualified Him to die in our place and require that He suffer a grueling death that caused His precious blood to be poured out for His people. All so we could get to know Him and He could abide or dwell with those who choose Him.

After supper he took another cup of wine and said, "This cup is the new covenant between God and his people—an agreement confirmed with my blood, which is poured out as a sacrifice for you (Luke 22:20 NLT)

His blood represents the new and better covenant that super-cedes the old one that came before. The blood of Jesus was poured out so we could live. That is the only thing that counts as far as God is concerned today.

And Jesus said to them, I assure you, most solemnly I tell you, you cannot have any life in you unless you eat the flesh of the Son of Man and drink His blood [unless you appropriate His life and the saving merit of His blood].

He who feeds on My flesh and drinks My blood has (possesses now) eternal life, and I will raise him up [from the dead] on the last day.

*For My flesh is true and genuine food, and My <u>blood</u> is
true and genuine drink.*

*He who feeds on My flesh and drinks <u>My blood</u> dwells continually in Me,
and I [in like manner dwell continually] in him.*

*Just as the living Father sent Me and I live by (through, because of) the
Father, even so whoever continues to feed on Me [whoever takes Me for his
food and is nourished by Me] shall [in his turn] <u>live through and because of
Me. (John 6:53-57 AMP)</u>*

Many have made a religion out of knowing about the Christ but a real Christian knows or will eventually learn that it is the personal relationship that counts. What Jesus is saying is that He lives only because of the living Father and we can only live through "taking Jesus for one's food and drink". He who would live eternally is he who will take Jesus into his innermost being.

When we do not have a good understanding regarding the "Main Thing" (knowing God in a very personal way) we can be misled into following other gods and doctrines (Gal.4:8-9). Anything that adds to or takes away from the "Main Thing" in any way is "another doctrine". God gave Himself for us in Christ and that is the Gospel. It has never been about anything we can ever do on our own. It has always been about our FAITH in believing He did it all for us by the shedding of His blood (as a sacrifice for our sin) when we were unable (because of our fallen condition) to do anything to help ourselves.

Any doctrine that says we need anything more than the blood of Jesus is false. Any belief or doctrine that says we have to do something in addition to just believing what was freely given to us as a gift from God (received by faith) is taking honor away from His sacrifice. Any teaching that says God is going to treat one people group differently than another dishonors the blood. Any belief based in keeping laws and ordinances given under the old covenant discredits the blood and debases the Son of God. The writer of Hebrews clearly states the seriousness of treating the blood with disrespect in any manner.

> *Any person who has violated and [thus] rejected and set at naught the*
> *Law of Moses is put to death without pity or mercy on the evidence of*
> *two or three witnesses. How much worse (sterner and heavier) punishment*
> *do you suppose he will be judged to deserve who has spurned and [thus]*
> *trampled underfoot the Son of God, and who has considered the*
> *covenant blood by which he was consecrated common and unhallowed,*
> *thus profaning it and insulting and outraging the [Holy] Spirit [Who*
> *imparts] grace (the unmerited favor and blessing of God)?*
> *(Hebrews 10:28-29 AMP)*

Prior to gaining a deeper understanding of "the Main Thing" I am sure that I was in violation of the above Scripture by allowing and supporting other teaching that treated the blood of Jesus with less reverence than it deserves. This was done unwittingly and out of ignorance. No more will I give place to any doctrine that does not honor the blood of Jesus in the highest sense.

There is a simple formula for the "Main Thing". It is as follows:

The blood of Jesus + anything else ='s NOTHING

The blood of Jesus + nothing ='s EVERYTHING

That secret (key) to greater understanding and intimate relationship with the God of Abraham, Isaac and Jacob is to discern that Jesus Christ is the unifying focus of all Scripture, not just the New Testament. He alone is the one, divinely ordained subject matter that synchronizes both the Old and New Testaments into one harmonious message, God's redemption plan for all mankind. The "Main Thing" truly is God's love story.

He and He alone is the "fundamental" key that has never and will never change.

The Main Thing

THE FUNDAMENTALS

Activity in the church today seems to be centered more on denominational theology and distinguishing belief systems, teaching and debates
over differences in interpretation, rather than endeavoring to practice the
most fundamental element of the game, the command of Christ "to love
Him with all our heart and love our neighbor as ourselves".

> *"You can't skip fundamentals if you want to be the best. Some guys are
> looking for instant gratification, so maybe they skip a few steps. It's like
> they're so focused on composing a masterpiece that they never master the
> scales. And you can't do one without the other. The minute you get away
> from fundamentals – whether it's proper technique, work ethic, or mental
> preparation – the bottom can fall out... Dean Smith taught me the game.
> He taught me the importance of fundamentals and how to apply them to
> my individual skills. I had that foundation to work from... You have to
> monitor your fundamentals constantly because the only thing that changes
> will be your attention to them. The fundamentals will never change. Get the
> fundamentals down and the level of everything you do will rise."*
> Michael Jordan 1

Few people would argue against the fact that success in any endeavor in life
is the refinement of basic principles that never change. We are witnessing
a lot of change in the world but when it comes to the fundamentals, they

never change. I think it is always prudent to post the definition of our subject so everyone is on the same page.

fun·da·men·tal (fŭn′də-mĕn′tl)

adj.

a. Of or relating to the foundation or base; elementary:

b. Forming or serving as an essential component of a system or structure; central:

n.

1. Something that is an essential or necessary part of a system or object.

Foundation of <u>reality</u>

So, fundamental means "the essential, elementary component of a system or object". My paraphrasing would be "the foundation of success" or "the basic principle that is necessary for accomplishment".

But my most favorite definition of fundamental is "the foundation of reality". You will understand why I say that in just a short while if you stay with me. But first, please allow me some further explanation regarding the importance of fundamentals.

Michael Jordan said it well. Certainly sports comprise only a portion of life events but they do serve as great illustrations. For example, let's take football. One could have the greatest stadium, the best looking uniforms and great players but all teams know that whoever controls the line of scrimmage is the team that usually wins. This basic principle (fundamental) never changes.

When I was young I loved athletics. I played football, basketball, baseball and golf. Each of those sports has essential elements (fundamentals of execution) that must be learned prior to engaging successfully at any level.

My favorite real life example of this comes from a time when I was talked into coaching my son's 3rd and 4th grade basketball team. I had been a player at the collegiate level but had no experience teaching the game to others, especially little guys who for the most part had never been involved in team sports and most of them had barely ever bounced a ball. For my team I ended up with a disproportionate number of 3rd graders to go with several 4th graders that were less desired by the other coaches. I did have my son who had some elementary skills developed from playing at home with me. There was only one small gymnasium to accommodate several leagues so our access to a court was limited to three, one-hour practice sessions prior to our first game.

At the basic level basketball is a game of running, shooting, passing, jumping, rebounding and coordinating in some organized fashion with teammates. You also have to learn how to keep the other team from scoring a reasonable amount of time if you are going to win games. How on earth can you make progress in a situation like this in such a short amount of time with so many things to learn and almost everyone starting from zero. Oh, I forgot to mention that I was still highly competitive and did not like to think about losing, especially to the other coaches in the league who had somehow stacked the deck in their favor to some degree.

So here is what we did. I am not sure to this day how it occurred to me but it did. I was put in mind that there is one boring, dull "fundamental" basketball function that governs all other aspects of the game. That function is "proper footwork". If one does not learn how to move his feet correctly it is next to impossible to properly position oneself for shooting, rebounding, playing defense and establishing the rhythm necessary to perform as a team. Much to the disappointment of the kids, instead of focusing on the "funner" things like shooting from the 3 point line and running plays, we spent the majority of our first practice learning how to shuffle our feet. This was not popular but the kids were hungry to learn and they sensed that I cared a lot about them as people so they trusted me and did what I asked. The second practice was more of the same. We did work a little on some basic offense and a few minutes of defensive alignment, but the majority of our time was focused on "footwork" drills. By the last practice, with everyone having some basic understanding of how to move properly, we were better able to communicate other necessary tasks with a greater degree of success.

In our first game we were pretty rough around the edges but it was clear that our group was built on the right foundation. The other guys had some players with advanced ability but were more clumsy and sporadic in their execution as a team.

Fast forward to the end of the season. I don't remember our exact record but against the odds we had won enough times to make it to the final game, playing for the league championship. The score was nip and tuck down to the last seconds. My son and my point guard, the only two players who could handle the ball very well had been fouled out of the game. We were losing by one point with just a few seconds left to play. The situation looked hopeless. My backup guard was a 3rd grader who was literally the smallest kid in the entire league. By all appearances, our hopes were sunk. We had called our last timeout and I had no choice but to have the ball inbounded to the 3rd grader. What happened next is right out of "Hoosiers". The ball was passed in to the 3rd grader and all I can remember is watching our hopes go down the tubes as he dribbled the ball to the opposite sideline from where I was coaching, but moving his little feet as he had practiced. I actually lost sight of him because his tiny frame was hidden by all the other bodies between him and the basket. As the last remaining seconds ticked off the clock, amazingly I saw the ball come arching up out of the pack toward the goal. In a heartbeat, the buzzer sounded as that ball swished the net for two points. Stunningly, we win the championship by one point in the last second of the game on the heroics of the most unlikely player in the entire league. I will never forget it. No it wasn't the Final Four or the NBA Finals but for the kids and I and the parents, it was pandemonium. No one could ever convince me that what happened in this scenario would have been possible if the kids had been unwilling to "practice the most basic, mundane, element of the game".

So what does a basketball game have to do with the Bible? Remember the earlier reference to my favorite definition of "fundamental", the foundation of reality?

I believe with all my heart that our approach to understanding Scripture and comprehending God's plan of redemption for mankind works exactly like that basketball team. There is one and only one governing "fundamental" of our faith that is the key to everything. When we get that fundamental down pat, the other aspects of the game will begin to fall into place.

Human nature is to take the path of least resistance. Unfortunately that can apply to our spiritual life as well. I think many Christians have a tendency to go with the flow and never really focus that heavily on the "fundamental foundation of our faith".

I ask at this point, "What is the most basic, foundational element of our faith as Christians"? Is it possible that we have a tendency to want to gravitate to other elements of the game before firmly establishing complete understanding of the one basic, essential building block that the entirety of Scripture and the anchor of our faith is "rooted and grounded" in, namely our Lord Jesus Himself. Maybe you don't agree that this happens. Listen to Jesus as He addresses the church of Ephesus in the 2nd chapter of Revelation:

I know your industry and activities, laborious toil and trouble, and your patient endurance, and how you cannot tolerate wicked [men] and have tested and critically appraised those who call [themselves] apostles (special messengers of Christ) and yet are not, and have found them to be impostors and liars.

I know you are enduring patiently and are bearing up for My name's sake, and you have not fainted or become exhausted or grown weary.

But I have this [one charge to make] against you: that you have left (abandoned) the love that you had at first [you have deserted Me, your first love].

Remember then from what heights you have fallen. Repent (change the inner man to meet God's will) and do the works you did previously [when first you knew the Lord], or else I will visit you and remove your lampstand from its place, unless you change your mind and repent.
(Revelation 2:2-5 AMP)

According to Jesus, the Ephesian church was deeply involved in Christ following activity and was in many ways functioning in worthwhile endeavors in His name. Firmly, He tells them they have wandered away from the fundamental aspect of the game and if they do not repent (have a change of heart) it is going to cost them. He is saying that they have left the original love relationship they had with Him in the beginning and allowed their focus to be shifted to the external elements of church life. He makes it clear to them that they need to recognize their mistake, repent (turn around on the inside) and bring their full attention back on the "love connection" with Him. Clearly He is saying that if you continue to stray from the fundamental, foundational element of the faith, (The Main Thing) you are in danger of losing big time.

Jesus says "I am the way, the truth and the life". Isn't that stating that He alone is the "foundation of reality" upon which everything true and right is built. Jesus was clearly telling the Church at Ephesus that salvation is in Him personally, not in all the things they could be doing in His name, no matter how conscientious they are about it(see Matt.7:21-23). Surely He alone is THE basic principle, the fundamental foundation from the beginning and for all time. Consider the following Scripture:

> *Jesus looked directly at them and asked, "Then what is the meaning of that which is written: "'The stone the builders rejected has become the cornerstone. Everyone who falls on that stone will be broken to pieces; anyone on whom it falls will be crushed."*
> *(Luke 20:17-18 NIV)*

> *Consequently, you are no longer foreigners and strangers, but fellow citizens with God's people and also members of his household, built on the foundation of the apostles and prophets, with Christ Jesus himself as the chief cornerstone. In him the whole building is joined together and rises to become a holy temple in the Lord. And in him you too are being built together to become a dwelling in which God lives by his Spirit.*
> *(Ephesians 2:19-22 NIV)*

> *For no one can lay any foundation other than the one already laid, which is Jesus Christ. (1 Corinthians 3:11 NIV)*

I am attempting to drive home the point that a large segment of Christianity over the years may have unwittingly strayed away from the fundamental. The Christian faith is heavily steeped in denominational doctrine that has been passed from generation to generation and the tendency may often be to just accept what "we have always believed" as truth without ever really drilling down on the "fundamental foundation of reality" that the entirety of Scripture is based on. If the cornerstone of our spiritual house (Jesus Christ) is not put in straight or gets turned around, our structure will be on shaky ground. Please allow me to use another personal analogy that is a true story.

Years ago, I decided that I was going to build a home on some land that I owned. I chose to be my own general contractor. I thought the most important initial concern was who I should hire to frame or build the basic structure of the house. The person I selected told me that he would not frame the house for me unless he also dug and poured the foundation for the house. He went on to explain that if the foundation was not put in right, it would be impossible for him to make corrections that would make the framing come out square, or right. It was that simple, flawed foundation, flawed house. That made a lot of sense to me then and it makes sense to me now. Not just with "earthly" buildings but even more importantly when we are constructing our "heavenly" domicile. Jesus is supposed to be the "chief cornerstone" of our building. He is the only foundation on which our spiritual house can be correctly constructed. If "the cornerstone" is not properly chiseled or set in its rightful place, our entire doctrine can be significantly flawed. If the real, complete truth of who Jesus is and what He has accomplished for us is misunderstood, not comprehended in entirety or has errors, the spiritual house can never be square or "right".

Remember that enemy of our soul that the Bible says exists only for the purpose of "killing, stealing and destroying" (John 10:10) the people God created. I believe his job is much easier when he is able to keep us from properly comprehending the full magnitude of "the foundation of all reality", Christ Jesus Himself.

In the secular world there is a question that gets asked often. "What is the most defining event in human history"? Even in the most material minded environments, almost always one will find Jesus Christ mentioned as one of the top ten answers given to this question.

Whether from a worldly or purely Christian perspective, without a doubt, the "most defining event" to ever occur in human history is the birth of Jesus Christ. Not only is He the "foundation of reality", Scripture says the entire universe is held together by the Word of His power. He is the unifying focal point of the entirety of Scripture. He is the cornerstone, the foundation, the one basic, fundamental key that must be properly discerned if one desires to know the "way, the truth and the life" God has hidden for us in Christ.

In this book, the spotlight is on Jesus Christ, our Lord and Savior, the basic principle of our faith that never changes.

> *Jesus Christ is the same yesterday and today and forever.*
> *(Hebrews 13:8 NIV)*

He is the true "promise of Abraham", the true Son of Abraham (Matt.1:1) the true "blessing of Abraham through whom we receive the promise of the Spirit" (Gal.3:14).

Jesus Christ is God Himself in the flesh. He is not just "The Cornerstone", He is much, much more than just the foundation!!!

MUCH MORE THAN A FOUNDATION

—⚬⚬⚬—

Prior to coming to a new place of understanding, I was misled (mostly from my former denominational interpretation and personal ignorance of the Word) into thinking that the ethnic nation of Israel, their land and the people were the "main thing", the central focus that Scripture was built upon and around. Without really ever taking notice to the contrary, I always just thought that the inheritance "promises" God gave to Abraham were made to him and his natural descendants forever. It never entered my thoughts that there was a natural Israel and a spiritual Israel and that they would not necessarily refer to the same people. It was when I started studying to gain more revelation about the "promise" to Abraham that many of my earlier beliefs regarding the natural, ethnic nation of Israel began to unravel. Who Jesus Christ is in relation to the "promises" made to Abraham is of critical importance in understanding the "Main Thing" of all Scripture. Consider the following regarding the magnitude and magnificence of our Lord Jesus Christ.

In the previous chapter, we saw Scripture clearly speaking that Jesus Christ is the "chief cornerstone" the "only foundation that has already been laid". The reality is that He not only is the foundation but without Him, the universe would come apart. Check out what it says:

> *For in him all things were created: things in heaven and on earth, visible and invisible, whether thrones or powers or rulers or authorities; all things have been created through him and for him.[7] He is before all things, and in him all things hold together*
> *(Col.1:16-17NIV)*

Jesus Christ, (The Word of God) created the universe, is over ALL things and sustains ALL things by "the power of His Word":

> *In the past God spoke to our ancestors through the prophets at many times and in various ways[2] but in these last days he has spoken to us by his Son, whom he appointed heir of all things, and through whom also he made the universe. The Son is the radiance of God's glory and the exact representation of his being, sustaining all things by his powerful word. After he had provided purification for sins, he sat down at the right hand of the Majesty in heaven*
> *(Hebrews 1:1-3NIV)*

Should we not give the most earnest heed to this passage? "Heir of **all** things". "The exact representation of God". "Sustaining **all** things by His powerful Word". In the past God spoke to our ancestors through the prophets but through the Son in these last days. We will discuss a little later where what He was speaking through the prophets was **all about** the Son. Jesus has always been the "Main Thing". We could post Scripture after Scripture that confirms that Jesus is everything and the only thing that matters in any context. Most Christians understand to some degree that the blood of Jesus saves us from sin. But how many ever really consider that the message of the entire Bible from Genesis through Revelation is all about God's **"promise"** for the redemption of mankind through the death, burial and resurrection of Jesus Christ, The Messiah?

Jesus said clearly that not knowing Scripture (He was speaking of the Old Testament at the time but I believe it applies today to both Old and New

Testaments and their relationship to one another) will result in erroneous and misguided theology (understanding of and relationship to God):

> *Jesus replied, "Your mistake is that you don't know the Scriptures, and you don't know the power of God. (Matthew 22:29 NLT)*

With 34,000 distinct denominations, there must be some erring and mistakes taking place. Maybe some of those different versions don't directly "trample on the Son of God" and "consider the covenant blood as common and unhallowed" (Hebrews 10:29) but I believe many do and never give it a thought. I consider it safe to think that if all those factions are "Christian" the distinctions must have something to do with conflicting viewpoints about "The Christ", who He Is, Was, and Is to be. I have been taught that counterfeit doctrine will always follow a guide that can be used to test against the truth. It is "add, subtract, multiply and divide".

1. ADD-If teaching adds anything to the Word of God, it is seriously in error. If one does not "know" what the Word actually says, it is much more difficult to avoid this trap. If Jesus is the Word of God (John 1:1) wouldn't adding something (to the Word) that is not there be changing something about Jesus, "the Main Thing"?

2. SUBTRACT-This fault occurs when the Deity of Christ is diminished or "taken away from" in any way. Jesus the man was God Himself in human flesh. Examine world religions to see what they say about Him. Test this against what many of the "Christian" denominations say. Any doctrine that would teach, suggest or imply that Jesus is anything other than God is false.

3. MULTIPLY-This major mistake occurs by increasing the requirements for salvation. Our salvation is based on nothing but faith in (The Christ) "the Main Thing". Nothing else we can **ever** do

in and of ourselves can gain us the Kingdom of God. Doing the will of God by following the commandments of Christ is our only mandate.

4. DIVIDE—False doctrine separates and divides the people. We have already visited that God's will is unity in Christ (the Main Thing). What is it that is impeding "one mind, one accord" unison in the Body of Christ today? Without question, it is disagreement among the numerous traditions founded on the Biblical interpretations of men passed down through the ages that have caught on as Christian doctrine. The Apostle Paul said that "Christ is not divided"(1Cor.1:13) and that the church is not to put up with any other Jesus (a different Gospel) than the one being preached (2 Cor.11:4). Division is the predictable result when there is misinterpretation or lack of knowledge concerning "the Main Thing".

Jesus said we make mistakes because we don't know the Scriptures. The people He was addressing were insulted and took offense because the Scriptures were what they studied and taught and was purported to be the basis for their "religion". I find it interesting how they could be so sup-posedly close to God's Word and yet so far away from the reality of "the Main Thing" Scripture is all about.

Most of what I believe were doctrinal errors on my part happened because of a lack of understanding of how "the Main Thing" (Christ) Jesus is interrelated with "the promise of Abraham" and the truth about His con-nection to the nation of Israel and the Old Testament. Biblical truths con-cerning the "Seed" of Abraham and the true heirs of "the promise" God made to him had somehow eluded me in the past.

Today it seems that all too often "the main thing" in many churches is teaching "what we believe" and "what rules and regulations" we are sup-posed to be following to be good members. Side note: In over fifty years in church, I do not remember ever hearing a sermon or teaching that presented Jesus Christ as the "Main Thing" from the entirety of Scripture perspective.

By not keeping the "Main Thing the main thing" we can be misled into believing doctrine that is not true Scripture. I have concluded that the majority of doctrinal disharmony in the Christian church today will in some way be related to the relationship of "the Main Thing" to Old Testament issues. Most established methods of Scriptural interpretation that I have studied (amillennial, premillenial, postmillennial, dispensationalism and covenant theology (to name a few) all engage eschatology (study of end time events) as a major focus of their attention. At the core of the debate among those viewpoints is the true disposition of the nation state of natural, ethnic Israel currently and at Christ's return at the end of the age and what happens from that point into the future.

Seldom do I hear that anyone in Christian circles believes we are not in the last of the last days. If that be the case, and I believe it is, that means that the second coming of Christ could be very near. If that is true, it seems that our focus should be more on "are we ready to meet Him" and "what will He find us doing at His return" than quarrelling among ourselves over the so called "nonessentials" of day to day church life. Before continuing, allow me to take a moment here to make a couple of statements. In no way am I anti-Semitic. I believe with all my heart that eternal life in heaven belongs to "whosoever believes in his heart that Jesus is the Christ" and that includes Jew and Gentile alike. I do not believe anyone has the authorization or the directive to tell someone else how they should believe and I am not writing for the purpose of doing so. I am saying that poring over the Bible from a "Main Thing" interpretive viewpoint makes a tremendous difference in bringing clarity to many difficult passages of Scripture, especially those dealing with the "spiritual" and "ethnic" Israel of God. Considering Christ as the long term redemption plan from "before the foundation of the world" and following that premise from Genesis to Revelation caused me to see ethnic Israel and the Jewish people in a much different light than I had ever considered before.

It begins with the "promises" to Abraham.

Jesus is the true "Seed" of Abraham (Gal.3:16), the promise of the Spirit that we receive through faith in Christ, the blessing promised by God to Abraham in the Genesis account.

Understanding "the promise" made to Abraham is critical to comprehending "the Main Thing".

THE PROMISE TO ABRAHAM

Most Christians are somewhat familiar with the Genesis account of how God creates man in His own image and gives him ruling power over the earth. Man falls prey to the deception of evil and unwittingly conveys his worldly dominion to satan. This tragic misuse of Adam's God given free will to choose resulted in mankind's separation from the Kingdom of God (His love). God told the serpent (devil or satan) that He (God) was sending a Herald that would crush his head and restore the Kingdom of God to earth and provide mankind the opportunity to return to God. God's promise to send a savior (the foundation our faith is built upon) who would redeem fallen mankind, restore the Kingdom of God and bring judgment on the "serpent who deceiveth the whole world" (Rev. 12:9) appears very early in Genesis.

And I will put enmity
Between you and the woman,
And between your seed and her <u>Seed</u>;
He shall bruise your head,
And you shall bruise His heel." (Gen. 3:15 NKJ)

Note: The "Seed of the woman" is a reference to a future descendant of Eve who would have no human father. Biologically, a woman produces no seed. Except for this one place, Biblical reference always speaks only of the seed of men. The promised Seed would, therefore, have to be supernaturally implanted in the womb. This is the only way He could avoid inheriting the sin nature which would disqualify every son of Adam from becoming a Savior from sin. This early prophecy certainly anticipates the future <u>virgin</u> birth of Christ.

Contrary to some teaching prevalent today within Christendom, this promise of a redeemer was made to ALL humankind and not just to one ethnic group of people. The "promise" is the <u>foundation, "the corner-stone"</u> of the Christian faith. The entirety of Scripture in some manner is all about "man's fall from God's grace and God's plan to redeem him back to Himself through the death, burial and resurrection of His Son Jesus Christ" (The Holy Seed).

God HAS reconciled us to Himself through Jesus Christ

> *And all of this is a gift from <u>God, who brought us back to himself through Christ.</u> And God has given us this task of reconciling people to him. For God was in Christ, reconciling the world to himself, no longer counting people's sins against them. And he gave us this wonderful message of reconciliation. (2Cor. 5:18-19 NLT)*

This Holy Seed, the Christ, while having Almighty God as His father must also have a human mother. God needed to establish a human lineage for His Son to be born into. God looked for a son of Adam who could be counted worthy to have his progeny bear the responsibility of carrying the "promise" in their genealogy. He found such a man in Abram (Abraham). Abraham was chosen for one reason only, his <u>FAITH.</u>

> *And he [Abram] <u>believed</u> in (trusted in, relied on, remained steadfast to) the Lord, and He counted it to him as righteousness (right standing with God).*
> *(Gen. 15:6 AMP)*

It was by faith that Abraham obeyed when God called him to leave home
and go to another land that God would give him as his inheritance. He went
without knowing where he was going. (Hebrews 11:8 NLT)

Nowhere in Scripture have I been able to find that Abraham was chosen because God wanted one special race of people to serve Him? Actually, Abraham was far from perfect but God regarded him as righteous because he deeply believed in and obeyed God, in other words, his **faith.** (Gen. 15:6, 22:18, 26:4-5, Romans 4:3, 20-22, Hebrews 11:8)

The basis for man's reconciliation with God has always been whether or not we choose to believe His Word, here again, our faith. **Faith is a huge deal to God!!!** Faith was the issue with Cain and Abel, way back early in Genesis.

By faith Abel brought God a better offering than Cain did. By faith he was
commended as righteous, when God spoke well of his offerings. And by faith
Abel still speaks, even though he is dead. (Hebrews 11:4 NIV)

From the very beginning, inheriting the promise comes through faith, not because one belongs to a "special" favored race of earthly, ethnic people. Faith is internal not external. The promise has always been of the spirit and not of the flesh.

Back to Abraham and the promise. God assured Abraham that he would be the father of a great nation and ALL peoples of the earth would be blessed in him (Abraham, not necessarily the nation of Israel). Abraham was never called Israel. (Gen. 12:2-3, 18:18)

"I will make you into a great nation,
and I will bless you;
I will make your name great,
and you will be a blessing.[a3 I will bless those who bless you,

> *and whoever curses <u>you</u> I will curse;*
> *and <u>all peoples on earth</u>*
> *will be blessed through <u>you</u> (Gen.12:2-3 NIV)*

Does this familiar passage say the blessing was to come from the nation or from Abraham personally? The promises were not made to Abraham's ethnic descendants but specifically to Abraham and "The Christ"?

> *Now to <u>Abraham and his Seed</u> were the promises made. He does not say,*
> *"And to seeds," as of many, but as of one, "And to <u>your Seed</u>,"^[a] <u>who is</u>*
> *<u>Christ</u>. (Gal.3:16 NKJ)*

The inheritance promises that God gave Abraham were made effective through Christ, Who is Abraham's true Seed (Matt. 1:1). These promises were not and cannot be made effective through sinful man's keeping of God's law. The promise of an inheritance is made only to those who have faith in Jesus, the True Heir of Abraham. All spiritual benefits are derived from Jesus and apart from Him there is no participation in the promises. Since Jesus is the Mediator of the Abrahamic Covenant, all who bless Him (Jesus) and His people will be blessed of God, and all who curse Him and His people will be cursed of God. These promises do not apply to any particular ethnic group but to the Church of Jesus Christ, the true Israel of God.

By the way, who would you say that the "peoples" of the world have been more blessed by, Christ (The SEED) or by the earthly nation of Israel?

Is Scripture clear that it was the Gospel of Christ that was being referred to in the promise to Abraham? The Apostle Paul says it is:

And the Scripture, foreseeing that God would justify (declare righteous, put in right standing with Himself) the Gentiles in consequence of faith, <u>proclaimed the Gospel</u> [foretelling the glad tidings of a Savior long beforehand] <u>to Abraham in the promise</u>, saying, In <u>you</u> shall <u>all the nations [of the earth] be blessed</u>. (Gal. 3:8 AMP)

This promise of Christ, The Holy Seed, who would redeem all mankind back to God was foreordained, or established, before the world began. (1 Peter 1:20, Ephesians 1:4, Rev. 13:8)

Blessed be the God and Father of our Lord Jesus Christ, who has blessed us with every spiritual blessing in the heavenly places in Christ, just as <u>He chose us in Him before the foundation of the world,</u> that we should be holy and without blame before Him in love
(Eph. 1:3-4 NKJ)

There are those today who are teaching Jesus (The Holy Seed, The Eternal Promise) was an afterthought or a Plan B after the nation of Israel's failure. I do not know what they do with the Scripture we just read.

The statement has been made that the entirety of Scripture is about the Christ. The truth is that: The entire Old Testament is concerning the promised Seed---**Jesus The Christ is coming!**

Revelations of Jesus are made throughout the Old Testament from Genesis to Malachi. In almost every book one will find some direct or indirect reference to the person or type of Christ. Consider this outline of Jesus in the Old Testament.

Jesus in the Old Testament

Outline and Scripture Verses only

"These are the Scriptures that testify about me," Jesus said in Jn.5:39.

Jesus taught that there were references to himself in the Old Testament.

In Jn.5:46, Jesus speaks specifically of Moses (the author of the first five books of the Old Testament) writing about him, "If you believed Moses, you would believe Me, for he wrote about me."

In Lu.24:13-27, Luke writes that Jesus taught the two disciples on the Emmaus road about himself from the OT. He writes in v.27, "And beginning with Moses and all the prophets, he explained to them what was said in all the Scriptures concerning himself."

What are the Old Testament references to Jesus, the messiah, the Son of God?

There are basically two kinds of OT references to the Son of God, the messiah.

They are the messianic prophecies and pre-incarnate appearances.

I. His Messianic Prophecies in the OT

A. OT prophecies of the messiah's true identity

1. The messiah was called by the titles of God, Jehovah and Elohim, in the OT.

a. Jehovah

1) Jehovah says to Zechariah that in the future the Jews "will look upon me whom they have pierced."

Zechariah 12:1-10 In v.10 Jehovah says that they will "look upon me whom they have pierced and mourn for him as one mourns for an only son."

This agrees with Ps.22:16 where David predicts that the messiah would be pierced when he says, "they pierced my hands and my feet."

In Rev.1:7 John writes of Jesus, the messiah, when he says, "Behold, he comes in the clouds; and every eye shall see him, and those also who pierced him and all the tribes of the earth shall mourn because of him."

2) Jeremiah 23:5-6 predicts that the messiah will be described by the divine name of Jehovah.

Jeremiah 23:5-6

b. Elohim

1) In Isa.9:6-7, Isaiah predicted that the messiah would be "mighty God."

2) In Isaiah 40:3, Isaiah predicted that the messiah would be coming would be the Lord God preceded by a herald.

3) In Isaiah 7:14, it is prophesied that the messiah would be "Immanuel," God with us.

The apostle Matthew by the inspiration of the Holy Spirit quotes this OT prophecy in Matt. 1:20-24.

4) In Ps.45:6-7, David's declaration of the divinity of the messiah, the coming king, points to the divinity of the messiah.

This verse is quoted in Hebrews 1 in reference to Jesus Christ.

c. Jesus accepts the OT titles of Jehovah and Elohim in the NT.

1) In several psalms, David addresses the Lord as his Lord and God. He personally worships God as deity.

Ps.7:1 Ps.13:3 Ps.30:1

This personal declaration by David to his Lord and God is the same one used by the apostle Thomas to Jesus Christ.

Jn.20:26-29, Thomas calls Jesus, "My Lord and my God."

d. Indirect references to Jesus as Jehovah and Elohim of the OT

1) There are NT passages where the author applies OT passages that are clearly referring Jehovah or Elohim to Jesus Christ.

In Heb.1:10-12 the author applies an OT passage, which teaches that God created the earth and universe to Jesus Christ. This is a quote from Ps.102:25-27 where the psalmist speaks of God's creation of the earth and universe.

2) In Eph.4:7-10, Paul applies to Jesus Christ an OT statement by David, which was addressed to God.

Paul quotes Ps. 68:18.

3) In John 12:41 John claims that Isaiah the prophet saw Jesus in his glory as the Lord God.

In Jn.12:41, John explains why many Jews saw Jesus' miracles, but still rejected him. He says that it was because of God's judgment which God himself had predicted would happen.

This was prophesied by Isaiah the prophet in Isa.6:9-10.

2. The messiah was prophesied to be both David's physical descendent and David's spiritual Lord in the OT.

It was predicted in the OT that the messiah would be the "Son of David," that is, a physical descendent of David who would "reign on David's throne."

See 2 Sam. 7:12-13, Ps. 89:3- 4, Isa.9:6-7

The Jewish leaders believed and taught this. See John 7:42

Jesus fulfilled this prophecy as he was the physical descendent of David through his mother Mary (Lu.1:27, 32) and the legal descendent of David through Joseph (Matt.1:1, 17, Lu.2:4).

Jesus accepted the title of "Son of David" which means that he accepted the people's recognition of him being the messiah. See Matt.9:27-31; 20:29-34; 21:14-16

In Matt.22:41-46, Jesus taught that messiah was predicted not only to be a human being descended from David, but also an eternal divine being who was superior to David. Jesus quotes Ps.110:1.

3. The messiah was prophesied to be the Son of God in the OT.

a. In Heb.1:4-5, the writer applies two OT texts to Jesus that speak of the messiah's true identity as the Son of God.

The first statement comes from Ps.2:7-12.

The second quote is from 2 Sam.7:13-14 and/or 1 Chron.17:12-13.

b. In Jn.1:49, Nathanael recognizes the supernatural knowledge that Jesus possesses and immediately calls him the "Son of God."

c. At his trial before the leaders of Israel, the high priest asks Jesus plainly if he is claiming to be "the Son of God." Jesus said "yes."

Matt.26:63-64

In Jn.20:30, John explains that he wrote his gospel to show Jesus is the Son of God.

4. The messiah was prophesied to be the Son of Man, the king, who will come to earth in power and glory and rule over it.

a. In the book of Daniel, God gave to Daniel a revelation of the messiah and Daniel referred to him as "son of man."

Dan.7:13-14

b. Jesus took upon himself this messianic title, "Son of Man" and referred to his fulfillment of this vision of messiah.

Mark13:24-27

Matt. 26:63-64

5. The messiah was prophesied to be the cornerstone and foundation of Israel.

Isaiah 28:16

Paul referred to this prophesy of Jesus in two passages.

Rom. 9:31-33 Eph. 2:20

Ps.118:22

Acts 4:11

I Peter 2:6-8

B. OT prophecies of the messiah's birth, ministry, death, resurrection, and eternal glory

1. The messiah's birth

a. The messiah would be born in Bethlehem.

Micah 5:2

Mat.2:3-6

b. The messiah would be born from a virgin

Matt.1:18-25

Isa:7:14

2. The messiah's ministry

a. The messiah would begin his ministry in Galilee

Mat.4:12-17

Isa.9:1-2.

b. The messiah would have a ministry of preaching and miracles.

Matthew 9:35

Isa.61:1-2

Lu.4:16-21

2) Jesus also applied another passage from Isaiah to himself, which predicts his healing ministry as he answers the question of the disciples of John the Baptist.

Mat.11:1-6.

Isa.35:3-6.

3. The messiah's suffering and death

a. Isaiah 53

b. Ps.22

Matt.27:46

4. The messiah's resurrection

a. The messiah would die and rise again from the dead.

Acts 2:22-32

Peter quotes Ps.16:8-11.

In Acts 13:34-37, Paul also appeals to this psalm as a prediction that Jesus, the messiah, would be resurrected from the dead.

II. His pre-incarnate appearances in the OT

A. The Son of God was called the Angel or Messenger of the Lord when he appeared in the OT.

In the Old Testament, a being appears who is called the "Messenger of the Lord" or the "Messenger of God" and is also called "Lord" and "God."

He is described as separate from the Lord (Jehovah) and yet is called Lord (Jehovah). He is described as separate from God (Elohim) and yet is called God (Elohim). This perfectly coincides with the how the Son of God is described in the New Testament.

The Hebrew word translated "angel" also means "messenger" (one who brings a message from another).

Although it is often translated as "Angel of the Lord." However, he is clearly not an angelic spirit being as can be seen from context of the various passages where he appears.

The appearances of the Son of God as the "Messenger of the Lord" in the OT are given below in chronological order.

1. The Messenger of the Lord, the Son of God, appears to Hagar in Gen.16:7-14

2. The Messenger of the Lord appears to Abraham when he was about to sacrifice Isaac Gen.22:9-19

3. The Messenger of God speaks to Jacob in a dream and calls himself God in Gen.31:11-13.

4. The Messenger of the Lord appears to Moses in the burning bush in Exod.3:1-6.

5. The Angel of the Lord appears to Gideon in Jud.6:11-22.

6. Other passages where the Son of God appears as the Angel or Messenger of Jehovah are

Gen. 48:15-16 Exodus 13:21 and Exodus 14:19 Judges 2:1-5 Jud.13:1-22 1

It seems obvious to me that the above referenced outline shows conclusively that Jesus was not only the foundation and cornerstone of the New Testament but of the Old Testament as well.

Mr. Jones includes Scripture where Jesus says Moses and all the prophets wrote about Him.

Consider the writing of Moses in the book of Numbers concerning the Holy Seed, referenced in the fourth oracle of Balaam

> *"I see <u>Him</u>, but not now;*
> *I behold <u>Him</u>, but not near;*
> *A <u>Star</u> shall come out of Jacob*
> *A <u>Scepter</u> shall rise out of Israel,*
> *And batter the brow of Moab,*
> *And destroy all the sons of tumult. (Numbers 24:17 NKJ)*

In Hebrews 11:26 we are told that Moses chose "reviling over the Gospel of Christ" instead of the treasures in Egypt.

> *He considered the contempt and abuse and shame [borne for] the Christ (<u>the Messiah Who was to come</u>) to be greater wealth than all the treasures of Egypt, for he looked forward and away to the reward (recompense).*
> *(Hebrews 11:26 AMP)*

Furthermore, Moses told the fathers that those who would not receive The Christ would "be destroyed from the people of God"

> *Thus <u>Moses said to the forefathers</u>, The Lord God will raise up for you a Prophet from among your brethren as [He raised up] me; Him you shall listen to and understand by hearing and heed in all things whatever He tells you.*
>
> *And it shall be that every soul that does not listen to and understand by hearing and heed that Prophet <u>shall be utterly[a] exterminated from among the people</u>. (Acts 3:22-23 AMP)*

The Jewish Patriarch, David, spoke of "The Christ" in numerous passages throughout the book of Psalm. One example:

Your throne, O God, is forever and ever;
A scepter of righteousness is the scepter of Your kingdom.[7] You love
righteousness and hate wickedness;
Therefore God, Your God, has anointed You
With the oil of gladness more than Your companions. (Psalm 45:6-7 NKJ)

David long ago knew that it was The Messiah (The promised Seed) who was to be the descendant that would inherit his kingdom (Israel) and would sit on the throne. He clearly knew that it was not to be an earthly kingdom. He understood this was an act of the spirit and not the flesh.

"Dear brothers, think about this! You can be sure that the patriarch David
wasn't referring to himself, for he died and was buried, and his tomb is still
here among us.[0] but he was a prophet, and he knew God had promised with
an oath that one of David's own descendants would sit on his throne. [31]David
was looking into the future and speaking of the Messiah's resurrection. He
was saying that God would not leave him among the dead or allow his body
to rot in the grave.

"God raised Jesus from the dead, and we are all witnesses of this.[3] Now he
is exalted to the place of highest honor in heaven, at God's right hand. And
the Father, as he had promised, gave him the Holy Spirit to pour out upon
us, just as you see and hear today. [34] For David himself never ascended into
heaven, yet he said,

'The Lord said to my Lord,
"Sit in the place of honor at my right hand
[35] until I humble your enemies,
making them a footstool under your feet."'[a][6] "So let everyone in Israel
know for certain that God has made this Jesus, whom you crucified, to be
both Lord and Messiah!" (Acts 2:29-36 NLT)

Isn't that what the angel Gabriel was instructed to tell Mary just before she became pregnant with Jesus:

> *But the angel said to her, "Do not be afraid, Mary; you have found favor with God. You will conceive and give birth to a son, and you are to call him Jesus. He will be great and will be called the Son of the Most High. <u>The Lord God will give him the throne of his father David,</u> and he will reign over Jacob's descendants forever; his kingdom will never end."*
> *(Luke 1:30-33 NIV)*

<u>ALL</u> God's Holy prophets foretold the promise of the coming Messiah

> *Thus has God fulfilled what He foretold by the mouth of <u>all the prophets,</u> that His Christ (the Messiah) should undergo ill treatment and be afflicted and suffer. (Acts 3:18 AMP)*

At the time of John the Baptist, many of the people were anticipating that Messiah, the Christ, would be coming. Evidently there were some who had heard of His coming from the prophets because they were looking for Him.

> *And as the people were in expectation, and all men mused in their hearts of John, whether he were the Christ, or not; (Luke 3:15 KJ)*

The promise of The Christ made to Abraham was passed to his son Isaac:

> *Live here as a foreigner in this land, and I will be with you and bless you. I hereby confirm that I will give all these lands to you and your descendants,[a] just as <u>I solemnly promised Abraham, your father.</u>[4] I will cause your descendants to become as numerous as the stars of the sky, and I will give them all these lands. And <u>through your descendants all the nations of the earth will be blessed.</u>[5] I will do this because Abraham listened to me and obeyed all my requirements, commands, decrees, and instructions."*
> *(Gen. 26:3-4 NLT)*

And then on to Isaac's son Jacob:

> *At the top of the stairway stood the LORD, and he said, "I am the LORD,*
> *the God of your grandfather Abraham, and the God of your father, Isaac.*
> *The ground you are lying on belongs to you. I am giving it to you and your*
> *descendants. ¹⁴ Your descendants will be as numerous as the dust of the earth!*
> *They will spread out in all directions—to the west and the east, to the north*
> *and the south. And all the families of the earth will be blessed through you*
> *and your descendants (Gen.28:13-14 NLT)*

Note: The New Testament is very clear that there is a true Israel ("children of promise") and another Israel who is not "true Israel" even though they can both claim to be descendants (Romans 9:6-9). Galatians 3:16 states clearly that the above promise was made to Abraham and his Seed (Jesus Christ) and definitely not to his physical descendants (seeds).

Take thought for a moment about those who teach today that the promised blessings of Abraham were made to and come through the earthly nation of Israel (seeds) who have clearly rejected the Christ (to whom the promise was made).

It is reported that there are over 7 billion people alive on the earth today. Census reports say that there are approximately 14 million of those people who call themselves Jewish. That calculates to .20 of 1%. Those same reports say that over 2 billion are Christian—almost 1/3 of the entire population of the earth. Which of those two groups of people best fit the description of the promises made to Abraham, Isaac and Jacob about "all the families of the earth will be blessed through you and your descendants"?

God was faithful to the covenant He made with Abraham, Isaac and Jacob who had kept covenant with Him. God fulfilled His promise to them by making them a nation and establishing them in the promised land.

The ONLY reason earthly Israel ever became a nation was because of the PROMISE God made to Abraham, Isaac and Jacob!

> *"After the LORD your God has done this for you, don't say in your hearts,*
> *'The LORD has given us this land because we are such good people!' No, it*
> *is because of the wickedness of the other nations that he is pushing them out*
> *of your way. It is not because you are so good or have such integrity that you*
> *are about to occupy their land. The LORD your God will drive these nations*
> *out ahead of you only because of their wickedness, <u>and to fulfill the oath he</u>*
> *<u>swore to your ancestors Abraham, Isaac, and Jacob.</u> [6] You must recognize that*
> *the LORD your God is not giving you this good land because you are good, for*
> *you are not—<u>you are a stubborn people.</u> (Deut. 9:4-6 NLT)*

God is merciful and longsuffering and endured much from the nation of Israel throughout their history. From the time of Abraham, Isaac and Jacob, they continually rebelled against God.

> *For I am the LORD, I change not; therefore ye sons of Jacob are not*
> *consumed. Even <u>from the days of your fathers ye are gone away from mine</u>*
> *<u>ordinances,</u> and have not kept them. Return unto me, and I will return unto*
> *you, saith the LORD of hosts. But ye said, Wherein shall we return?*
> *(Malachi 3:6-7 KJ)*

He made it clear from the beginning, however, that their physical existence as a nation and as His people was conditional on them keeping covenant with Him.

> *Then GOD's Message came to me: "Can't I do just as this potter does, people*
> *of Israel?" GOD's Decree! "Watch this potter. In the same way that this*
> *potter works his clay, I work on you, <u>people of Israel</u>. At any moment I may*
> *decide to pull up a people or a country by the roots and get rid of them. But if*
> *they repent of their wicked lives, I will think twice and start over with them.*
> *At another time I might decide to plant a people or country, but <u>if they don't</u>*

> *cooperate and won't listen to me, I will think again and give up*
> *on the plans I had for them. (Jer. 18:5-10 MSG)*

Moses told the Israelites what would happen if they turned their hearts away from God.

> *But if your heart turns away so that you do not hear, and are drawn away,*
> *and worship other gods and serve them, I announce to you today that you shall*
> *surely perish; you shall not prolong your days in the land which you cross over*
> *the Jordan to go in and possess. (Deuteronomy 30:17-18 NKJ)*

Joshua told the Israelites that God had fulfilled ALL the promises He had made to them. He then told them the same thing God had spoken through Moses that would happen to them if they did not keep covenant with the Lord.

> *If you violate the covenant of the LORD your God, which he commanded you,*
> *and go and serve other gods and bow down to them, the LORD's anger will*
> *burn against you, and you will quickly perish from the good land he has given*
> *you." (Joshua 23;16 NIV)*

Scripture and history both record that the nation of Israel did indeed perish from the land and was scattered into other people groups. Although they were gathered back several times, Jerusalem was "utterly destroyed" in 70 AD and the Jews were dispersed into other nations. Noteworthy that this happened within a generation after the "appearing of Shiloh" (the Messiah-the Promise) to receive the authority for the rule and reign of the Kingdom of God that has been His from the beginning.

> *The scepter or leadership shall not depart from Judah, nor the ruler's staff*
> *from between his feet, until Shiloh [the Messiah, the Peaceful One] comes to*
> *Whom it belongs, and to Him shall be the obedience of the people.*
> *(Gen. 49:10 AMP)*

The same verse, a different translation:

> *The sceptre shall not depart from Judah, nor a lawgiver from between his feet,*
> *until Shiloh come; and unto him shall the gathering of the people be.*
> *(Genesis 49:10 KJ)*

As Dr. Henry M. Morris' *The Defender's Bible* explains:

"This important prophecy has been strikingly fulfilled. Although Judah was neither Jacob's firstborn son nor the son who would produce the priestly tribe, he was the son through whom God would fulfill His promises to Israel and to the world. The leadership, according to Jacob, was to go to Judah, but this did not happen for over 600 years. Moses came from Levi, Joshua from Ephraim, Gideon from Manasseh, Samson from Dan, Samuel from Ephraim and Saul from Benjamin. But when David finally became king, Judah held the scepter and did not relinquish it until after Shiloh came. "Shiloh" is a name for the Messiah, probably related to the Hebrew word for "peace" (shalom) and meaning in effect, "the one who brings peace."

According to the Jewish historian Josephus, the Sanhedrin of Israel lost the right to truly judge its own people when it lost the right to pass death penalties in 11 A.D. (Josephus, Antiquities, Book 17, Chapter13). Jesus Christ was certainly born before 11 A.D. 2

Abraham, Isaac, Jacob, Moses, David and all of God's holy prophets recognized that the promise of the Messiah (Shiloh) was to come through the nation of Israel. Obviously, the earthly nation of Israel, and specifically the tribe of Judah, would therefore need to remain intact until the prophecy concerning the Christ (the Promise) could be fulfilled. Jacob foreknew that all authority (the scepter) has belonged to "Messiah" from the very beginning. Jacob says that the leadership (the scepter) would remain in Judah until Messiah appears. The "scepter" was entrusted to the earthly nation of Israel because they were the descendants of Abraham, Isaac and Jacob. Ethnic Israel provided the earthly, human channel necessary for the Christ to "come in the flesh". Genesis 49:10 indicates that (the scepter) departed from Judah upon His arrival because " the One to whom it has always belonged" has now appeared on the scene to assume His rightful position as King and Lord (Redeemer) of all who will believe in Him"?

Despite all this Scriptural evidence to the contrary, there are many teaching today that earthly, physical Israel (Judaism) still maintains a distinctive role in God's redemption plan on the basis that they are His chosen, "special" favored race of earthly, ethnic people. In other words, He has a separate covenant for Jews than for everybody else. As previously stated, the promise was always spiritual and not of the flesh.

> *For he is not a [real] Jew who is only one outwardly and publicly, nor is [true] circumcision something external and physical.²⁹ But he is a Jew who is one inwardly, and [true] circumcision is of the heart, a spiritual and not a literal [matter]. His praise is not from men but from God.*
> *(Romans 2;28-29AMP)*

Once again from another place:

> *He redeemed us in order that the blessing given to Abraham might come to the Gentiles through Christ Jesus, so that by faith we might receive the promise of the Spirit. (Galatians 3:14 NIV)*

One more time spoken a little differently:

> *It doesn't matter whether we have been circumcised or not. What counts is whether we have been transformed into a new creation.⁶ May God's peace and*

> *mercy be upon all who live by this principle; they are the new people of God.*
> *(Gal. 6:15-16 NLT)*

Repeating for emphasis, ethnicity has never been a factor in God's plan. Faith in His Word has always been His way and it remains so to this very day. "The just shall live by faith".
(Habakkuk 2:4, Romans 1:17, Gal. 3:11, Heb. 10:37)

> *Look at the proud; his soul is not straight or right within him, but the [rigidly] just and the [uncompromisingly] righteous man shall [a] live by his faith and in his faithfulness. (Habakkuk 2:4 AMP)*

One last time just to make sure this is unmistakably clear:

> *Clearly no one who relies on the law is justified before God, because "the righteous will live by faith."[a] The law is not based on faith; on the contrary, it says, "The person who does these things will live by them."[b] Christ redeemed us from the curse of the law by becoming a curse for us, for it is written: "Cursed is everyone who is hung on a pole."[c] He redeemed us in order that the blessing given to Abraham might come to the Gentiles through Christ Jesus, so that by faith we might receive the promise of the Spirit. (Gal. 3:11-14 NIV)*

Abraham is mentioned prominently in God's list of faithful servants in Hebrews. Yet we read that neither he nor those faithful who came after him (Hebrews 11:12-13) have yet to receive the fulfillment of the promise of the eternal inheritance God made to him. (Heb. 11:39-40.)

> *And all of these, though they won divine approval by [means of] their faith, did not receive the fulfillment of what was promised, Because God had us in mind and had something better and greater in view for us, so that they [these heroes and heroines of faith] should not come to perfection apart from us [before we could join them].*
> *(Heb. 11:38-40 AMP)*

Who then inherits the promise and when?

> *Therefore know that <u>only those who are of faith</u> are sons of Abram.*
> *(Gal. 3:7 NKJ)*

The promise made to Abraham of eternal life in Christ Jesus has been made available to everyone who believes in Him. It has nothing to do with race, sex, or national origin. All who are of promise are one in Christ. (Gal.3:28-29)— **There is no special race of people that are favored by God over another because of ancestory!**

> *There is [<u>now no distinction</u>] neither Jew nor Greek, there is neither*
> *slave nor free, there is not male [a]and female; for you are <u>all one in Christ</u>*
> *<u>Jesus</u>[9] And if you belong to Christ [are in Him Who is Abraham's Seed],*
> *then you are Abraham's offspring and [spiritual] heirs according to promise*
> *(Gal. 3:28-29 AMP)*

Therefore it is true Christians who are living along with God's people from throughout history who served Him in faith (looked forward to the coming Christ) who are the heirs of the promise. All people of faith (in the promise of the Christ) will receive the spiritual, eternal promise at the same time.

> *For the Lord Himself will descend from heaven with a loud cry of summons,*
> *with the shout of an archangel, and with the blast of the trumpet of God.*
> *And those who have departed this life in Christ will rise first.[17] Then we, the*
> *living ones who remain [on the earth], <u>shall simultaneously be caught up along</u>*
> *<u>with [the resurrected dead]</u> in the clouds to meet the Lord in the air; and so*
> *always (through the eternity of the eternities) we shall be with the Lord!*
> *(1 Thess. 4:16-17 AMP)*

THE PROMISE TO THE NATION OF ISRAEL

There is much debate in Christian communities today over the inheritance promises that God made to Abraham and how those promises relate to the present day nation of Israel and the Jewish people. There are those who say that God has made "promises" to the physical Israel that have not yet been fulfilled. I believe that this issue needs to be addressed in this work because of its strong connection to "the Main Thing" thematic and the issues surrounding the spiritual and ethnic seed of Abraham. Let's take a close look. To the best of my understanding, the promises made to Abraham, Isaac and Jacob were The Seed, the nation many descendants and the land.

The majority of Christian professing people I know anything about agree that the Seed, (The Christ) and the Nation and many descendants have been fulfilled. That leaves the land as the only promise allegedly not fulfilled.

What does the Bible say regarding the land promise to earthly Israel?

- It was to be given to Israel "forever" (Gen. 13:15) and as "an everlasting possession" (Gen. 17:8)

All the land that you see I will give to you and your offspring[a] forever.
(Gen.13:15 NIV)

• And again:

The whole land of Canaan, where you now reside as a foreigner, I will give as
an everlasting possession to you and your descendants after you;
and I will be their God." (Gen. 17:8 NIV)

Was this promise fulfilled?

According to Joshua 21:43-45, God GAVE the land, Israel possessed the
land and lived in the land. Verse 45 is very clear that ALL things spoken
to the house of Israel "came to pass".

So the LORD gave Israel all the land he had sworn to give their ancestors,
and they took possession of it and settled there. [44] The LORD gave them
rest on every side, just as he had sworn to their ancestors. Not one of
their enemies withstood them; the LORD gave all their enemies into their
hands. [45] Not one of all the LORD's good promises
to Israel failed; everyone was fulfilled.
(Josh. 21:43-45 NIV)

Joshua states it again in 23:14-15—here he says "all good things the Lord
promised you have come upon you". He goes on to prophesy to them that
they will perish quickly and be "utterly destroyed" from the land because
they would not keep the covenant.

"It's almost time for me to die. You know and fully believe that
the LORD has done great things for you. You know that he has not failed to
keep any of his promises. Every good promise that the LORD your
God made has come true, and in the same way, his other promises will come

true. He promised that evil will come to you and that he will destroy
you from this good land that he gave you.
(Josh. 23:14-15 NCV)

Does God keep His promises? I think He does---ALWAYS. Was Israel faithful to God or were they continually rebellious? The promise to RECEIVE the land was <u>unconditional </u>but:

- The promise to RETAIN the land was <u>conditional</u>

"But if your heart turns away and you refuse to listen, and if you are drawn
away to serve and worship other gods,[18] then I warn you now that you will
certainly be destroyed. You will not live a long, good life in the land you are
crossing the Jordan to occupy. (Deut.30:17-18 NLT)

And what about Jeremiah 18:9-10 that we saw earlier, different translation this time:

O house of Israel, can I not do with you as this potter does? says the Lord. Behold, as the clay is in the potter's hand, so are you in My hand, O house of Israel.

At one time I will suddenly speak concerning a nation or kingdom, that I will pluck up and break down and destroy it;

And if [the people of] that nation concerning which I have spoken turn from their evil, I will relent and reverse My decision concerning the evil that I thought to do to them.

At another time I will suddenly speak concerning a nation or kingdom, that I will build up and plant it;

And if they do evil in My sight, obeying not My voice, then I will regret and reverse My decision concerning the good with which I said I would benefit them. (Jer. 18:6-10 AMP)

Do you see a problem here? We seem to have "dueling" Scriptures. In some places it says Israel will occupy the land forever and in another it says they will be "destroyed" from the land. So why does it say that the land was given to the nation of Israel "forever" if they were going to be displaced from it? If God always keeps His promises what about that "everlasting" and "forever" arrangement?

The Hebrew word that is translated as "forever" and "everlasting" in those passages is <u>OLAM</u>.

In researching the Hebrew word "olam", I have found that it actually means "in the far distance" instead of a time that never ends. It is used frequently for time in the distant past or the distant future as a time that is difficult to know or perceive. References that I have seen say that it is mistranslated often in English to mean "forever", a time that never ends. This same reference says that the Hebrew of the Old Testament Scriptures has no term that carries the concept of eternity. "Olam" simply means "long duration", "antiquity", "futurity", "until the end of a period of time". Whatever the period of time is must be determined by context.

Sometimes the use of "olam" means only "an age" and sometimes "only up to the end of a man's life" (Samuel's life in 1 Sam. 1:22, 2:35 and David's lifetime in 1 Sam. 27:12; 28:2). In these cases, the English is "forever" but from context it is clearly speaking only of the time until the end of that man's life.

Deuteronomy 23:3 says "forever" but limits the term to ten generations. So the context here is "of an age". In 2 Chronicles 7:16, it translates as "forever" but describes just the period of the first Temple. So the word "forever" in Hebrew does not mean the same thing as "forever" means in English. Olam just means "up to the end of a period of time". Other examples of the use of the same word are as follows:

Many ordinances of Mosaic law such as circumcision, Passover, the priesthood of Aaron, many feast days, animal sacrifice, etc. were given as everlasting and forever (olam). If everlasting always meant forever then we should still be observing these ordinances even though the New Testament teaches that they were not permanent.

If God had obligated Himself by His covenant of promise to establish the natural seed of Abraham in the land "forever", wouldn't that have been a breach of covenant on His part to pluck them from off the land and scatter them among all the nations of the world?

There is a land that God promised Abraham that he and his descendants would inherit and that land promise does last forever!!

> *[Urged on] by faith Abraham, when he was called, obeyed and went forth to a place which he was destined to receive as an inheritance; and he went, although he did not know or trouble his mind about where he was to go.*
>
> *[Prompted] by faith he dwelt as a temporary resident in the land which was designated in the promise [of God, though he was like a stranger] in a strange country, living in tents with Isaac and Jacob, fellow heirs with him of the same promise.⁰ For he was [waiting expectantly and confidently] looking forward to the city which has fixed and firm foundations, whose Architect and Builder is God. (Hebrews 11:8-10 AMP)*

Does anyone believe that the city Abraham saw in the "promise" is the earthly Jerusalem? Isn't this very clearly speaking to the "Jerusalem above" mentioned by Paul in Galatians 4:26?

Abraham and a multitude of his descendants all died not having received the promise of the city but were looking forward to it!!

So from one man, though he was physically as good as dead, there have sprung descendants whose number is as the stars of heaven and as countless as the innumerable sands on the seashore. These people all died controlled and sustained by their faith, but not having received the tangible fulfillment of [God's] promises, only having seen it and greeted it from a great distance by faith, and all the while acknowledging and confessing that they were strangers and temporary residents and exiles upon the earth. Now those people who talk as they did show plainly that they are in search of a fatherland (their own country).⁵ If they had been thinking with [homesick] remembrance of that country from which they were emigrants, they would have found constant opportunity to return to it.⁶ But the truth is that they were yearning for and aspiring to a better and more desirable country, that is, a heavenly [one]. For that reason God is not ashamed to be called their God [even to be surnamed their God—the God of Abraham, Isaac, and Jacob], for He has prepared a city for them.(Hebrews 11:12-16 AMP)

That city they were promised and were looking for is the same city we are looking for!!

But rather, you have come to Mount Zion, even to the city of the living God, the heavenly Jerusalem, and to countless multitudes of angels in festal gathering,³ and to the church (assembly) of the Firstborn who are registered [as citizens] in heaven, and to the God Who is Judge of all, and to the spirits of the righteous (the redeemed in heaven) who have been made perfect,⁴ And to Jesus, the Mediator (Go-between, Agent) of a new covenant, and to the sprinkled blood which speaks [of mercy], a better and nobler and more gracious message than the blood of Abel [which cried out for vengeance]. (Hebrews 12:22-24 AMP)

All those descendants who are redeemed through their faith in the promise are waiting in Heaven while we who are still on earth wait for the "city of promise", the same heavenly Jerusalem they were looking for!

Then one of the seven angels who had the seven bowls filled with the seven final plagues (afflictions, calamities) came and spoke to me. He said, Come with me! I will show you the bride, the Lamb's wife.

Then in the Spirit He conveyed me away to a vast and lofty mountain and exhibited to me the holy (hallowed, consecrated) city of Jerusalem descending out of heaven from God, (Rev.21:9-10 AMP)

"The promise" has always been about "the heavenly Jerusalem, not the earthly one!!

She is like Mount Sinai in Arabia and is a picture of the earthly city of Jerusalem. This city and its people are slaves to the law. ²⁶ But the heavenly Jerusalem, which is above, is like the free woman. She is our mother. It is written in the Scriptures:

"Be happy, Jerusalem.
You are like a woman who never gave birth to children.
Start singing and shout for joy.
You never felt the pain of giving birth,
but you will have more children
than the woman who has a husband."

My brothers and sisters, you are God's children because of his promise, as Isaac was then.
(Gal. 4:25-28 NCV)

The unconditional promise of the "earthly" land was made to Abraham, Isaac and Jacob and to their descendants. Scripture states clearly that every promise God made to the forefather's, which included the "earthly" land, was fulfilled. The promise to KEEP the "earthly" land was conditional? The Israelites would forfeit the "earthly" land if they turned to other gods which they did continually. When God said that the natural seed of Abraham would "perish" from the "earthly" land and be "utterly destroyed" and dispersed into other nations because of their continuous sin and rebellion, the only hope there would ever be for them would be to come to Christ. There are those that believe that God has a different plan for followers of Judaism (Jews) and the present day nation of Israel. That would mean a separate covenant (Mosiac) would remain in place for a small group of people that rivals God's plan of redemption in Christ that was put in place before the foundation of the world. Doesn't the New Testament teach us clearly that it was necessary that the old covenant and all of the foreshadowing of Christ connected with it from the Old Testament should pass away to make a place for "the new and better covenant established on better promises?

> *But as it now is, He [Christ] has acquired a [priestly] ministry which is as much superior and more excellent [than the old] as the covenant (the agreement) of which He is the Mediator (the Arbiter, Agent) is superior and more excellent, [because] it is enacted and rests upon more important (sublimer, higher, and nobler) promises.*

> *For if that first covenant had been without defect, there would have been no room for another one_or_an attempt to institute another one.[8] However, He finds fault with them [showing its inadequacy] when He says, Behold, the days will come, says the Lord, when I will make_and_ratify a new covenant_or_agreement with the house of Israel and with the house of Judah.*

> *It will not be like the covenant that I made with their forefathers on the day when I grasped them by the hand to help and relieve them and to lead them out from the land of Egypt, for they did not abide in My agreement with them, and so I withdrew My favor_and_disregarded them, says the Lord*

> *For this is the covenant that I will make with the house of Israel after those days, says the Lord: I will imprint My laws upon their minds, even upon their innermost thoughts and understanding, and engrave them upon their*

hearts; and I will be their God, and they shall be My people. And it will nevermore be necessary for each one to teach his neighbor and his fellow citizen or each one his brother, saying, Know (perceive, have knowledge of, and get acquainted by experience with) the Lord, for all will know Me, from the smallest to the greatest of them.

For I will be merciful and gracious toward their sins and I will remember their deeds of unrighteousness no more.[13] When God speaks of a new [covenant or agreement], He makes the first one obsolete (out of use). And what is obsolete (out of use and annulled because of age) is ripe for disappearance_and_to be dispensed with altogether. (Hebrews 8:6-13)

Questions:

- If the promise of a Messiah (the new covenant) was established before the creation of the world and His coming was preached to Abraham and foretold by Moses, David and Jacob, and also by ALL the prophets throughout the Old Testament, why was He rejected by the religious leadership and unbelieving Jewish people of His day who supposedly were/are experts on the Old Testament and why is it no different today?

- The above passage of Scripture refers to a new covenant that God is making with the House of Israel. He says it will be entirely different from the old covenant. What is the "new" covenant He is talking about if not the blood covenant established by Jesus Christ, the Messiah, the promise of Abraham? . How can the "House of Israel" not be referring to all the people of God under the new covenant instead of the "earthly" nation of Israel in Palestine who, if anything, has chosen to remain in the old covenant that clearly has been replaced?

- If Judaism, the Jewish religion of the earthly nation of Israel has rejected the promise of the new covenant through the Messiah, and the old has passed away, what "Scriptural" covenant are they operating under today?

- How does God "engrave His laws upon man's heart" except by the indwelling of the Holy Spirit available ONLY through Jesus Christ. If Christ (God) is rejected, how do Jews (Judaism) connect with God?

So here's my problem. The promise that a Redeemer would come to rescue mankind was foreordained before the world was created. The message was communicated to Abraham and his immediate descendants and ratified by Moses and David and all the Prophets. The "earthly" nation of Israel was to carry the message until the Redeemer appears. After He comes all authority is to now rest in Him. Emanuel (God with us) comes to earth to live in human form, suffers and dies a horrific death on the cross and then is resurrected. His payment in full of our debt of sin reconciles us back to God (Himself). How does it make any sense that God (The Word in John 1:1) would institute a new and superior covenant to replace the old and facilitate it Himself by "becoming flesh and dwelling among us" (John 1:14) only to somehow need or desire to acknowledge the old inferior covenant now or sometime in the future because some Jewish people refuse to believe? As a Christian, I find it impossible to believe that the plan of God to redeem mankind back to Himself, facilitated completely by Himself (Christ) and currently in place for almost 2,000 years applies to all the nations of the world except the nation of Israel. It seems ludicrous to me that God would have a separate plan (covenant) in place for just one small people group that differs from His plan in Christ. Please help me understand how that would not be favoritism on God's part.

Is our God a "respecter of persons" or one who shows "partiality"? I think the Word teaches different.

NO RESPECTER OF PERSONS

———— ⊶⊷ ————

*And He has <u>made from one blood</u> every nation of men to dwell on
all the face of the earth (Acts 17:26 NKJV)*

par·ti·al·i·ty

unfair bias in favor of one thing or person compared with another;
favoritism.

synonyms: <u>bias</u>, <u>prejudice</u>, <u>favoritism</u>, <u>favor</u>, <u>partisanship</u>

Millions of Christians today unconditionally support the earthly nation of
Israel and Jewish people as the "chosen of God" on the basis of a special distinction they believe God has made toward them and with them
because of a connection they believe them to have with ancient Hebrew history. I have no purpose or agenda to want to believe differently than those
brothers and sisters. I was raised on the dispensational viewpoint and just
accepted it as truth so it would be so much easier to try to defend it than to
change my perspective. However, the more I study the Bible with a "Main
Thing" perspective, the harder it is to make those "pieces" fit together.

We have already looked at Scripture that clearly tells us that the promise
made to Abraham was to Abraham and to his SEED who is Jesus. Over

and over again we see that Jesus is the only way, truth and life there is. Salvation comes only through faith in The Christ. Current day Israel and non Christian Jewish people refuse to accept God's plan of redemption in Christ that is available to "all nations". They say the Gospel of Jesus Christ does not apply to them. They say they and they alone are the children of Abraham. Does God indeed have a favorite group of people that He has made a special exception for? If the answer to that question is yes, would that not be "unfair bias in favor of one thing or person compared to another"? How could that not mean that God is demonstrating "prejudice, favoritism, favor and partisanship" to Jewish people over everyone else? Please consider the following preponderance of Scripture that states plainly that God does not operate that way. He is not partial to or a respecter of any persons:

"For the LORD your God is the God of gods and Lord of lords. He is the great God, the mighty and awesome God, who shows no partiality and cannot be bribed. (Deut.10:17 NLT)

How is giving non-believing Jewish people special privilege with regard to their salvation differing from the plan established before the foundation of the world or giving them and only them a second chance to "get it right" not contradictory to this Scripture and all that follows in this segment?

And Peter opened his mouth and said: Most certainly and thoroughly I now perceive and understand that God shows no partiality and is no respecter of persons (Acts 10:34 AMP)

If Jewish people are treated differently than the rest of the world, how is that not special treatment of persons and in direct opposition to this entire body of Scripture?

For God shows no partiality¹ undue favor or unfairness; with
Him one man is not different from another].
(Rom. 2:11 AMP)

Here we see more contradiction by those that say God is treating Jewish people differently with regard to their rejection of His plan in Christ, that He has a separate plan for them than for the church (Dispensationalists). How does He implement such a plan and stay in conformity with His Word that says He does not deal with mankind in that manner?

Moreover, [no new requirements were made] by those who were reputed to be something—though what was their individual position and whether they really were of importance or not makes no difference to me; God is not impressed with the positions that men hold and He is not partial and recognizes no external distinctions—those [I say] who were of repute imposed no new requirements upon me [had nothing to add to my Gospel, and from them I received no new suggestions].(Gal. 2:6 AMP)

The Gospel of Jesus Christ is for both Jew and Gentile and there is no distinction between them. They are to be one in Christ. (Gal.3:28, Col. 3:11, Rom. 10:12). Anything else has to be partiality and respecter of persons!

You masters, act on the same [principle] toward them and give up threatening and using violent and abusive words, knowing that He Who is both their Master and yours is in heaven, and that there is no respect of persons (no partiality) with Him. (Eph. 6:9 AMP)

This truth is continuously repeated. Again I ask, how is it possible to have different covenants with different classes of people without showing partiality?

But if you do what is wrong, you will be paid back for the wrong you
have done. For <u>God has no favorites</u>.
(Col. 3:25 NLT)

Some Christians say that God has one redemption plan for the church of
Jesus Christ and a separate one for Jewish Israel. If true, wouldn't these
passages have to be misprints or errors in the Word?

But the wisdom that is from above is first pure, then peaceable, gentle, and
easy to be intreated, full of mercy and good fruits, <u>without partiality</u>, and
without hypocrisy. (James 3:17 KJV)

This truth seems clear and consistent.

And remember that <u>the heavenly Father to whom you pray has no favorites</u>.
He will judge or reward you according to what you do. So you must live in
reverent fear of him during your time as "foreigners in the land."
(1 Peter 1:17 NLT)

This is getting a bit redundant, would you agree?

They asked Him, Teacher, we know that You speak and teach what is right,
and that <u>You show no partiality to anyone</u> but teach the way of
God honestly and in truth. (Luke 20:21 AMP)

The dispensational theological viewpoint is that God has made a distinction between Jewish people and everybody else. They say He has a special connection to them that functions differently and separately from the
entire New Testament message of Christ that is "the only way, truth and
life" for everyone else except Jewish people. Their premise is that God has
one covenant with the church (comprised from ALL nations) and a different one with unbelieving Jews (Judaism). If that is not showing "partiality" and being a "respecter of persons" what is it? Scripture says showing

favor to one person over another is a sin that breaks God's royal law of love. How would it be a sin for us and not for God?

> *This royal law is found in the Scriptures: "Love your neighbor as you love yourself." If you obey this law, you are doing right. But if you treat one person as being more important than another, you are <u>sinning</u>. You are guilty of <u>breaking God's law</u>. (James 2:8-9 NCV)*

In light of the numerous passages we have just worked through, it seems clear to me that to have a secondary covenant plan in place for one small, ethnic group of people would not only defy Scriptural accuracy but would challenge the very just, fair and righteous nature of God.

WHO IS THE TRUE ISRAEL OF GOD

But far be it from me to glory [in anything or anyone] except in the cross of our Lord Jesus Christ (the Messiah) through Whom the world has been crucified to me, and I to the world!

For neither is circumcision [now] of any importance, nor uncircumcision, but [only] a new creation [the result of a new birth and a new nature in Christ Jesus, the Messiah].

Peace and mercy be upon all who walk by this rule [who discipline themselves and regulate their lives by this principle], even upon the [true] Israel of God!
(Galatians 6:14-16 AMP)

In the realm of Christianity today, a great deal of the disagreement and controversy among professing believers in Christ arises from the differences in how Scripture is to be interpreted. One huge division is over who is the "true Israel" of God. One opinion says it is Jesus Christ and His Body, the church, while others believe it to be the ethnic nation of Israel, its people and the land. Christian academia is overflowing with books and articles, websites and sermons about the different stances taken over "the Israel of God". One's Biblical interpretative viewpoint is considered to be his "theology".

A work attempting to magnify the risen Christ as the "Main Thing" of Biblical truth as its goal unfortunately cannot avoid a discussion of theology. I would much prefer it if we could because differences in one's "theology" is a root cause of divisions and factions among brothers and sisters in Christ today. One may not even be conscious that he is involved with the term but be assured that it is very unusual not to have some way of thinking about God. Even atheism must be a form of theology because it involves who God is or is not.

The Freedictionary.com description of <u>theology</u> is:

The study of the nature of God and religious truth; rational inquiry into religious questions. A system or school of opinions concerning God and religious questions:

So our "theology" is the basic <u>"schools of opinion"</u> regarding religious truth we hold to in forming our "beliefs" about the nature of God and what He desires us to know about Him and His Kingdom.

When theology involves Biblical Scripture, academia has a big word they use to describe one's approach to interpretation methodology. That word is <u>hermeneutics.</u>

her·me·neu·tics   (hûr´mə-n$\overline{oo}$´t$\breve{\text{i}}$ks, -ny$\overline{oo}$´-)

The <u>theory</u> and <u>methodology</u> of interpretation, especially of scriptural text.

Again, if God and the Bible are a part of one's life, it is very difficult to not be connected in some way with this concept. Please note <u>"hermeneutics"</u> is characterized as <u>"theory"</u> and <u>"methodology"</u>. Biblical truth was never intended to be reduced to man's theory or man's interpretation. We are supposed to be led into all truth by the Holy Spirit.

But the Comforter (Counselor, Helper, Intercessor, Advocate, Strengthener, Standby), the Holy Spirit, Whom the Father will send in My name [in My place, to represent Me and act on My behalf], He will teach you all things. And He will cause you to recall (will remind you of, bring to your remembrance) everything I have told you. (John 14:26 AMP)

Is it possible to think that oftentimes we are staunch defenders of man's "theories" and interpretive "methodologies" instead of just listening to the Holy Spirit in our hearts?

But you have received the Holy Spirit, and he lives within you, in your hearts, so that you don't need anyone to teach you what is right. For he teaches you all things, and he is the Truth, and no liar; and so, just as he has said, you must live in Christ, never to depart from him.
(1 John 2:27 TLB)

We are encouraged to "work hard" (with all diligence) to know and understand God's Word and what it means.

Work hard so God can say to you, "Well done." Be a good workman, one who does not need to be ashamed when God examines your work. Know what his Word says and means. (2 Tim.2:15 TLB)

I have heard directly from others and read many times that as long as you have Jesus somewhere in the "theological" mix you have the "essential" and it really doesn't matter what you believe when it comes to the "non-essentials". I really don't know what non-essentials are but I think they may be those other ideas Christians argue and fight over that turn into "dissensions", "factions" and "divisions". According to the following scripture, the church is expected to operate in perfect unity with regard to doctrine and not to have differing opinions.

*But I urge and entreat you, brethren, by the name of our Lord Jesus Christ,
that all of you be in <u>perfect harmony</u> <u>and full agreement in what you say,</u>
and that there be <u>no dissensions</u> <u>or factions</u> <u>or divisions among you,</u> but
that you <u>be perfectly united in your common understanding and in your</u>
<u>opinions</u> <u>and judgments</u>. (1 Cor. 1:10 AMP)*

From what I have been able to determine, there are two major "interpretative methodologies" that are most prevalent in Christian ideology
today. They are labeled "Dispensational" and "Covenant" theology. The
primary differences between the two involve "who is the true Israel of
God"? Naturally there are offshoots and combinations of these theories
that make understanding which "school of opinion" most closely resem-
bles "the one true Gospel" all the more difficult. To my reasoning, when
our search for truth is "impartial" and entirely centered in Jesus, it makes
what Scripture is saying to us more comprehendible. It is not the purpose
of this work to go into elaborate detail about Dispensational and Covenant
theology. I do believe it to be highly relevant to the "Main Thing" perspective to have a working knowledge of the primary differences between
the two viewpoints.

The first and most widespread is Dispensationalism.

*"Dispensationalism is a system of theology that has two primary distinctives. 1) A
consistently literal interpretation of Scripture, especially Bible prophecy. 2) A distinction
between Israel and the church in God's program. Dispensational theology teaches that
there are <u>two distinct peoples of God: Israel and the church.</u> Dispensationalists believe
that salvation has always been by faith—in God in the Old Testament and specifically
in God the Son in the New Testament. Dispensationalists hold that <u>the church has not</u>
<u>replaced Israel</u> in God's program and the Old Testament promises to Israel have not
been transferred to the church. They believe that the promises God made to Israel (for
land, many descendants, and blessings) in the Old Testament will be ultimately fulfilled
in the 1000-year period spoken of in Revelation chapter 20. Dispensationalists believe*

that just as God is in this age focusing His attention on the church, He will again in the future focus His attention on Israel (Romans 9-11).

Using this system as a basis, dispensationalists understand the Bible to be organized into seven dispensations: Innocence (Genesis 1:1–3:7), conscience (Genesis 3:8–8:22), human government (Genesis 9:1–11:32), promise (Genesis 12:1–Exodus 19:25), law (Exodus 20:1–Acts 2:4), grace (Acts 2:4–Revelation 20:3), and the millennial kingdom (Revelation 20:4-6). Again, these dispensations are not paths to salvation, but manners in which God relates to man. Dispensationalism, as a system, results in a premillennial interpretation of Christ's second coming and usually a pretribulational interpretation of the rapture. To summarize, dispensationalism is a theological system that emphasizes the literal interpretation of Bible prophecy, recognizes a clear distinction between Israel and the church, and organizes the Bible into the different dispensations it presents.

Covenant Theology views the covenants of Scripture as manifestations of either the Covenant of Works or the Covenant of Grace. The entire story of redemptive history can be seen as God unfolding the Covenant of Grace from its nascent stages (Genesis 3:15) through to its fruition in Christ. Covenant Theology is, therefore, a very Christocentric way of looking at Scripture because it sees the OT as the promise of Christ and the NT as the fulfillment in Christ. Some have accused Covenant Theology as teaching what is called "Replacement Theology" (i.e., the Church replaces Israel). This couldn't be further from the truth. Unlike Dispensationalism, Covenant Theology does not see a sharp distinction between Israel and the Church. Israel constituted the people of the God in the OT, and the Church (which is made up of Jew and Gentile) constitutes the people of God in the NT; both just make up one people of God (Ephesians 2:11-20). The Church doesn't replace Israel; the Church is Israel and Israel is the Church (Galatians 6:16). All people who exercise the same faith as Abraham are part of the covenant people of God (Galatians 3:25-29)." 1

It should be obvious which of these two methodologies this writer most closely associates with. I found a good excerpt that concisely summarizes the essence of covenant theology much better than I could say it. I believe it also echoes what I have been endeavoring to convey as "the Main Thing" in all of Scripture.

> *Everyone is in covenant with God and the sanctions are according to which covenant you are in. <u>Covenants are the architectural framework, the superstructure of the Bible.</u> Covenant theology <u>is just biblical theology</u> because we find covenants everywhere in the Bible. Many scholars try to discover what is the center of the Bible ... the center of biblical theology? Some of the proposed centers for biblical theology are <u>God, Israel, Covenant, creation, kingdom, salvation, new creation, and so forth.</u> None of these are the center of the Bible though. <u>They lose their meaning without Christ. If there is no Christ, there is no kingdom to talk about.</u> The diversity of the Bible is <u>unified in Christ. He is the center that holds all of the biblical data together.</u> While the covenants might be the vehicle by which God relates to his people and the kingdom of God is certainly his pervasive rule over all people yet <u>the fullest expression of God and His glory come in the person and work of the Lord Jesus Christ</u> and this is why covenants are important.*
> *They teach us about Him.*
> *- Rev Dan McManigal 2*

As the Scriptures are searched from a "Main Thing" interpretative perspective, it is difficult to ignore that there are two Israel's, one earthly and physical and the other spiritual. Distinguishing between the two can be difficult and may require unrelenting effort and seeking with an impartial, whole-hearted tenacity to discern the difference. We have just referenced two Christian doctrines today that involve sharp disagreement over which Israel is being referred to in any given passage of Scripture in both Old and New testaments. Dispensationalism maintains that God has "two separate and distinct covenants in place (two separate people of God), one with the earthly and physical Israel (Jews) and the other with the spiritual people of God established on the blood of Jesus recognized as the church or Body of Christ. Others including myself accept as true that all believers are God's children by the new birth and it is they who are the "true Israel of God" and they alone are the heirs of the promises made to Abraham and his Seed, the Christ.

I do not mean to disrespect the belief system that anyone chooses to accept. I have stated previously that no one has the right to tell anyone what doctrine they should believe. I think we each do have the right to share what we believe and to give the reasons for why we think our version is the truth. That has been my intention for this work from the outset. I also believe that we are expected to "get it right" with regard to "the Main Thing". Can there really be two "main things", Jews and Christians sharing the world stage as the "elect, chosen people of God". You will decide for yourself but I am suggesting that if there IS only one Israel, following after and supporting the wrong one could be getting dangerously close to conflicting with the following passage in Hebrews that we have looked at once before, different translation this time:

> *[8] For anyone who refused to obey the law of Moses was put to death without mercy on the testimony of two or three witnesses. [29] Just think how much worse the punishment will be for those who have <u>trampled</u> on the Son of God, and have <u>treated the blood of the covenant, which made us holy, as if it were common and unholy</u>, and have insulted and disdained the Holy Spirit who brings God's mercy to us.(Hebrews 10:28-29 NLT)*

No one that I know who calls themselves Christian would knowingly, or on purpose set their hearts to "trample on the Son of God or treat His shed blood as common and unholy". That doesn't mean it can't happen.

Let me post an example of what I am talking about. I have had several brothers and sisters (professedly in Christ) tell me that one's doctrine is not really that important as long as it recognizes Jesus. They have said it is much more important for all of us with different ways of perceiving Him to just be more accepting of one another's point of view and all of us just get along together. I am all in for us coming into agreement but here is where I see a problem. One of those individuals I am speaking of is an ordained, professing Christian minister who councils and has spiritual influence over other people, perhaps some who do not yet understand very much about the Gospel of Christ. This person has made the statement that "Jesus is the Messiah but He alone does not make us Holy". One of this person's close associates, also a Christian counselor, told me that Jesus is the Messiah but there is more to it than that. Both of these people were referring to "living a Torah observant" (following and attempting to keep the Mosaic Law) lifestyle in addition to the blood of the Messiah.

I would like to propose a very hypothetical question here. Just suppose for a moment that you (the reader) had an only son and that son was the apple of your eye. He was as close to being the perfect child as it gets. It is not possible to measure the love you have in your heart for him. However, you also love God and put Him first in your life. God speaks to you one day and says that if He could find someone with a near perfect son who would consider giving him up as a sacrifice for sin in the world, all of mankind would be able to just receive that unthinkable gift on your part and thereby be totally free from the legal requirements (laws) of a holy and just God. Through faith in and believing and receiving this selfless gesture, undeserving people everywhere could now be brought back into right standing with God. One person (your son) is being offered the opportunity to pay once and for all time, the sin debt that separated the loving God from His creation since the fall of Adam. Your heart sinks with the thought of the sacrifice but somehow you see the future glory that will enshroud your son for eternity and you agree. You are forced to endure the agony that accompanies the physical torture your son must suffer as he is ravaged by the dark forces of evil that break his body and spill his blood. But it is his shed blood that makes everyone free. Finally, it is done. Now you wait to experience the supreme appreciation that surely will be forthcoming from the people for the marvelous sacrifice made on their behalf by you and your son. Surely they will be filled with overflowing love for someone who would lay down his life in this manner for people he did not know personally.

You could never have imagined the actual response from humankind. Instead of love for your son, much of the world disdains the sacrifice you and he made to set them free. One particular, very small group of people claims to be related to your family tree and they say that your son's surrendering his life was not ordered by God. They say you must have been mistaken in what you thought you heard from THEIR God because they are accepted or rejected by God on the basis of their works, not according to anything you think your son accomplished. They and much of the religious community you are a part of also believe that these people are special to God just because of their alleged genealogical connection to your historic family.

Then there are still others who say they receive and recognize the sacrifice made on their behalf but they tell you they still need to follow the laws that God told you no human being could keep which is why He needed you to give up your son in the first place.

Now the question, do you think the actions of these people would be "trampling" on your son? Would you feel like his blood that God said would make them Holy was being treated as common? Would you feel insulted or have contempt for those people? I can't speak for you but I certainly think I know how I would feel. I know this scenario is not possible with people but it is with God and it is surely what He experiences through the sacrifice of His Son.

Now please correct me if I am in error here. My understanding is that the justice of God requires perfect obedience to the law. The fact that sinful man was/ is incapable of perfect obedience is why it took the shed blood of God Himself (The Christ) to redeem us back to Him. We can only be made Holy by receiving His free gift to us by faith. If that statement is true, and I believe it is "the Gospel truth", how can one be following and/or teaching that the blood requires anything else on our part without violating and contradicting the very Gospel it professes to believe?

I am no one's judge. However, in light of what the passage we have been referring to in Hebrews 10 says about "trampling on the Son and treating His blood as common", coupled with Galatians 5:4 where Paul says "you have become estranged from Christ, you who <u>attempt</u> to be justified by law, you have fallen from grace" makes it clear to me that <u>doctrine does matter</u> in the purest sense. How is it that these two aforementioned people (as sincere and well intentioned as they may be) and all who share their zeal for trying to keep the old Mosaic law (or follow any form of legalistic religion for that matter) are not confusing the two Israel's and attempting to follow after the physical earthly Israel and the old covenant that clearly has been replaced by the newer spiritual one that takes precedent?

You will have to come to your own conclusion but my concern is that misunderstanding of the two Israel's (unwittingly or otherwise) can lead to "trampling on the "Main Thing" and insulting the Holy Spirit.

I am unable to believe in any way shape or form that there is now or has ever been more than one people of God, His "true Israel".

Consider what some revered men of the past and present have to say about this issue:

Justin Martyr on "the true spiritual Israel" [6]

Jesus Christ ... is the new law, and the new covenant, and the expectation of those who out of every people wait for the good things of God. For the true spiritual Israel, and the descendants of Judah, Jacob, Isaac, and Abraham (who in uncircumcision was approved of and blessed by God on account of his faith, and called the father of many nations), are we who have been led to God through this crucified Christ. 3

John Calvin on Galatians 6:16 [10]

Upon the Israel of God. This is an indirect ridicule of the vain boasting of the false apostles, who vaunted of being the descendants of Abraham according to the flesh. There are two classes who bear this name, a pretended Israel, which appears to be so in the sight of men, and the Israel of God. Circumcision was a disguise before men, but regeneration is a truth before God. In a word, he gives the appellation of the Israel of God to those whom he formerly denominated the children of Abraham by faith (Galatians 3:29), and thus includes all believers, whether Jews or Gentiles, who were united into one church. 4

Martin Luther on Galatians 6:16

[1]*Lectures on Galatians, 1519.*[8] *"Walk" is the same verb that is used above (5:25). "Walk," that is, go, by this rule. By what rule? It is this rule, that they are new creatures in Christ, that they shine with the true righteousness and holiness which come from faith, and that they do not deceive themselves and others with the hypocritical righteousness and holiness which come from the Law. Upon the latter there will be wrath and tribulation, and upon the former will rest peace and mercy. Paul adds the words "upon the Israel of God." He distinguishes this Israel from the Israel after the flesh, just as in 1 Cor. 10:18 he speaks of those who are the Israel of the flesh, not the Israel of God. Therefore peace is upon Gentiles and Jews, provided that they go by the rule of faith and the Spirit.*

Lectures on Galatians, 1535.[9] *"Upon the Israel of God." Here Paul attacks the false apostles and the Jews, who boasted about their fathers, their election, the Law, etc. (Rom. 9:4-5). It is as though he were saying: "The Israel of God are not the physical descendants of Abraham, Isaac, and Israel but those who, with Abraham the believer (3:9), believe in the promises of God now disclosed in Christ, whether they are Jews or Gentiles." 5*

O. Palmer Robertson on the Israel of God [13]

The recognition of a distinctive people who are the recipients of God's redemptive blessings and yet who have a separate existence apart from the church of Jesus Christ creates insuperable theological problems. Jesus Christ has only one body and only one bride, one people that he claims as his own, which is the true Israel of God. This one people is made up of Jews and Gentiles who believe that Jesus is the promised Messiah.6

It appears to me that these men all very clearly believe that there is only one true Israel today and that it is "God's children by the new birth, both Jews and Gentiles who along with their father Abraham believe in the promises of God fulfilled in Christ Jesus". In fact, they seem to agree that Scripture speaks plainly that it is not the physical descendants of Abraham after the flesh that comprise "God's Israel.

The Apostle Paul says that the revelation God gave him about the church unlocked a mystery which had been hidden in God since the beginning of the world, namely, that all of God's people, whether Jews or Gentiles by natural descent were to be members of the same body.

> *As I briefly wrote earlier, God himself revealed his <u>mysterious plan</u> to me. ⁴ As you read what I have written, you will understand my insight into <u>this plan regarding Christ.</u> ⁵ God did not reveal it to previous generations, but now by his Spirit he has revealed it to his holy apostles and prophets.*
>
> *⁶ And <u>this is God's plan</u>: Both <u>Gentiles and Jews who believe the Good News</u> share equally in the riches inherited by God's children. <u>Both are part of the same body, and both enjoy the promise of blessings because they belong to Christ Jesus.</u>[a]((Ephesians 3:3-6 NLT)*

Clearly, that same body must be "the new Israel", the church. God has expressed His faithfulness to the Israel of the Old Testament in Christ Jesus!

Check this out in Revelation:

*After this I saw <u>a vast crowd</u>, too great to count, <u>from every nation and</u>
<u>tribe and people and language,</u> standing in front of the throne and before the
Lamb. They were clothed in white robes and held palm branches in their
hands.(Rev.7:9 NLT)*

The commonwealth of Israel now contains both Gentile and Jew. Those
who are citizens of the Israel of Old but who had not received Christ are
simply unsaved members of one of the many nations of the world.

*³ For I could wish that I myself were cursed and cut off from Christ for the sake
of my people, those of my own race,⁴ the people of Israel. Theirs is the adoption to
sonship; theirs the divine glory, the covenants, the receiving of the law, the temple
worship and the promises. ⁵ Theirs are the patriarchs, and from them is traced the
human ancestry of the Messiah, who is God over all, forever praised![a] Amen.*

God's Sovereign Choice

*⁶ It is not as though God's word had failed. For <u>not all who are descended from Israel</u>
<u>are Israel.</u> ⁷ Nor because they are his descendants are they all Abraham's children.
On the contrary, "It is through Isaac that your offspring will be reckoned."[b] ⁸ In
other words<u>, it is not the children by physical descent who are God's children</u>, but it is
the children of the promise who are regarded as Abraham's offspring. (Romans 9:3-9
NIV)*

These verses seem really straightforward to me. Clearly, the promises
were not made to the physical descendants of Abraham but to Abraham's
descendant who is Christ.

⁶ Now the promises (covenants, agreements) were decreed and made <u>to</u>
<u>Abraham and his Seed</u> (his Offspring, his Heir). He [God] does not say,
And to seeds (descendants, heirs), as if referring to many persons, but, And to
your Seed (your Descendant, your Heir), <u>obviously referring to one individual,</u>
<u>Who is [none other than] Christ (the Messiah).</u> (Gal.3:16 AMP)

According to David Holwerda in *Jesus and Israel* (p 30) "the Bible uses
"Israel" as the more common designation of the true people of God, His
elect community, the people of His covenant". He continues with:

"The people to whom God makes promises must be the people who
receive the promises. The Israel of promise must be the Israel of fulfillment. Interestingly, this is precisely where the New Testament begins."

The book of the genealogy of Jesus Christ, the <u>Son of David</u>, the <u>Son of Abraham</u>
(Matt. 1:1 NKJ)

According to Holwerda, Matthew, "by proclaiming Jesus as the Son of David
and Son of Abraham is not only announcing a new creation or new human-
ity, but a fulfillment of Genesis 12 and 2 Samuel 7. A new age has indeed
begun, new because after centuries of Israel's failure, the promises of God to
Abraham and David are finding their fulfillment in **their** Son, Jesus Christ."

"God's covenant with Abraham lays the foundation for the entire
ensuing history of redemption recorded in Scripture. By link-
ing Jesus to Abraham, Matthew is declaring that God's promise of blessing for the nations is now being fulfilled through Jesus.
(Gen. 12:2-3, 17:7, 22:18)."

"Jesus is what a true descendant of Abraham is supposed to be. <u>He</u>
<u>then is the true Israel,</u> the one who does everything Israel was sup-
posed to do and who is everything Israel is supposed to be. Historical
Israel had failed. <u>The promises</u> could not come to fulfillment through
them."

"Isaiah had declared that though Israel had become as numerous as "the sand of the sea", only <u>a remnant</u> would return (Is.10:22). Matthew now proclaims that the judgment of Israel by exile finds its answer and hope in the birth of Jesus ("from the deportation to Babylon to the Messiah, fourteen generations" Matt. 1:17)."

"<u>Jesus is the REMNANT</u> who represents the hope and rebirth of Israel announced by the prophets. <u>He is Israel, Abraham's Son.</u>"

"whose stump remains when it is cut down. So the <u>Holy Seed shall be its stump</u> <u>(Is. 6:13)</u>"

"There shall come forth a rod (shoot) <u>from the stem</u> (trunk) of Jesse and a Branch shall grow out of His roots" (Is.11:1) (Author's addition)

Holwerda continues by saying, "Jesus is more than His ancestry could produce. He represents the intervention of God, the creative work of the Holy Spirit which was active once in creation and was promised again in the messianic salvation of the end time. God provided what human history could not. In Christ, Emmanuel, God Himself has taken the place of His covenant partner (physical descendants of Abraham, Isaac, and Jacob) in order to secure the continuity of His covenant with Israel (God's elect or "chosen people"). **Israel can never again be defined apart from Jesus Christ"** 7

I would like to state again that my purpose is not to denigrate any group of people. It is my intention to magnify the Lord Jesus Christ. I do not believe He is exalted in any way by sharing His rightful place with anyone who refuses to recognize Him for what He is, the fulfillment of the promise of Abraham, the true Israel of God. Scripture very clearly reveals in numerous passages that there are two Israel's, one is spiritual and is represented by the "children of promise". The other Israel is said to be "of the flesh" and are not heirs of God (Gal.4:22-31). How is it that Bible believing people read those truths differently and say that God has two Israel's that are both God's people? If there really is only one people of God (in

Christ), how does one teach that there is another and not take glory away from all that Jesus Christ "is, was, and is to be"?

What is it that has caused so many people to believe that after Christ had come that the Jewish people remained "the Israel of God"?

The heart of the support people use for there being a distinctive future for a separate, ethnic Israel is found in the 11th chapter of Romans. In verses 25 and 26, that seems to those people to be what Paul is meaning when he says "all Israel will be saved". But if we take a deeper look, that interpretation has many problems.

All Israel Will Be Saved

[5] I do not want you to be ignorant of this mystery, brothers and sisters, so that you may not be conceited: Israel has experienced a hardening in part until the full number of the Gentiles has come in, [26] and in this way[a] <u>all Israel</u> will be saved.
As it is written:
"The deliverer will come from Zion;
he will turn godlessness away from Jacob. (Romans 11:25-26 NIV)

What Paul is saying deserves a closer look. In his book "The Israel of God" O. Palmer Robertson examines these verses and considers the possibilities of whom Paul is referring to as "all Israel". He says five possibilities have been proposed. They are as follows:

1. *All ethnic descendants of Abraham*
2. *All ethnic descendants of Abraham living when God initiates a special working among the Jewish people*
3. *The mass of Jews living at the time of a special activity of God*
4. *All elect Israelites within the community of Israel*
5. *Both Jews and Gentiles who together constitute the Church of Christ, the Israel of God*

1. *All ethnic descendants of Abraham.*

   a. *Scripture gives no hint anywhere that there is a "second chance" for salvation after death so this assertion must be rejected.*

2. *All ethnic descendants living when God does his special work.*

   a. *This is perhaps the most popular view today, that "all Israel" refers to the mass or majority of Jews living when the hardening of part of Israel is lifted.*

   b. *If this were accurate "all Israel" would refer broadly to the nation as a whole but not necessarily to every individual in the nation. In this case "all" can hardly mean "most". The hardening in verse 25 refers to the historical outworking of reprobation (rejection by God; the state of being condemned to eternal misery in Hell).*

   c. *As Paul says, the principle of hardening means that, "God gave them a spirit of stupor, eyes so that they could not see and ears that they could not hear". (Rom. 11:7-8). If a day is coming when the reprobation is lifted from Israel, then every single Israelite living at that time will be saved. If even one Israelite of that period is lost, then the principle of hardening or reprobation would still be active.*

   d. *This would mean that someday "every" living Israelite will come to salvation. God has never obligated Himself to save every single individual in any group of people. He has always saved individuals in and among those externally organized into a covenant community.*

   e. *If this pattern were changed in the future, it would introduce a principle foreign to all of God's previous redemptive activity, including activity under the gracious new covenant.*

3 *Every single Israelite living at some time in the future.*

   a. *The major problem here is how one identifies who is an Israelite. Who exactly is to be included in "all Israel"*

b. *The previous assumptions are made based on Jewish being defined on some form of ethnic basis. This assumption must now undergo serious scrutiny. Benno Jacob, the noted Jewish commentator on Genesis, insists that ethnic descent was not the ultimate basis for determining participation in the old covenant. He says: "differences of race have never been an obstacle to joining Israel which did not know the concept of the purity of blood. Circumcision turned a man of foreign origin into an Israelite." (Ex.12:48)*

c. *When God set aside Abraham as his instrument of blessing for the world, it was made plain that any Gentile could join the covenant community through the process of proselytism (Gen.17:12-13). Furthermore, no legislation in Israel forbade the marriage of an Egyptian proselyte to an Assyrian proselyte. The offspring of such a union would be fully Israelite, yet completely non-Abrahamic in ethnic origin. On the other hand, any descendant of Abraham might be declared a non Israelite if he violated the covenant (Gen.17:14). For these reasons, Israel could never be defined along purely ethnic lines.*

4 *All elect Israelites within the community of Israel. This would mean that all those identified with Judaism will one day be saved.*

a. *That would mean that a person could reject the Gospel of Christ, convert to Judaism and be assured of eternal life if he were living at the time when the special, mighty working of salvation of "all Israel" takes place.*

b. *If all Jews will someday be saved and if one can become a Jew by proselytism, then why would Christians not be encouraging people to become Jewish if they are unwilling to receive the message of Christ?*

c. *The idea that "all Israel" refers specifically to ethnic Jews is fraught with problems*

5 *Both Jews and Gentiles who together constitute the Church of Jesus Christ, the true "Israel of God"? 8*

All the New Testament and the efforts of this writer in this work emphasizes # 5 as the principal, "Main Thing" message of reality. (Author's addition)

MORE PROBLEMATIC SCRIPTURE FOR SEPARATE
PEOPLES OF GOD
(TWO SEPERATE ISRAELS)

⁹ Do not lie to each other, since you have taken off your old self with its practices ¹⁰ and have put on the new self, which is being renewed in knowledge in the image of its Creator. ¹¹ Here <u>there is no Gentile or Jew,</u> circumcised or uncircumcised, barbarian, Scythian, slave or free, but <u>Christ is all, and is in all.</u>

¹² Therefore, <u>as God's chosen people,</u> holy and dearly loved, clothe your selves with compassion, kindness, humility, gentleness and patience (Col.3:9-12 NIV)

How is this passage misunderstood? It so clearly says that those to be renewed, God's chosen people consist ONLY of both Jew and Gentile (no longer referred to in those two terms) but who have now become one in Christ!

And all who have been united with Christ in baptism have put on Christ, like putting on new clothes.[a] <u>There is no longer Jew or Gentile,</u>[b] slave or free, male and female. For you are <u>all one in Christ Jesus.</u> ²⁹ And now that you belong to Christ, <u>you are the true children</u>[c] <u>of Abraham.</u> You are his heirs, and <u>God's promise to Abraham belongs to you.</u> (Gal. 3:27-29 NLT)

The wall of separation between Jew and Gentile (the veil) was broken down by Christ and they were considered to be ONE PEOPLE forever.

⁴ For Christ himself has brought peace to us. <u>He united Jews and Gentiles into one people</u> when, in his own body on the cross, <u>he broke down the wall of hostility that separated us.</u> ¹⁵ He did this by ending the system of law with its commandments and regulations. He made peace between Jews and Gentiles by <u>creating in himself one new people from the two groups.</u> ¹⁶ <u>Together as one body, Christ reconciled both groups to God</u> by means of his death on the cross, and our hostility toward each other was put to death. (Ephesians 2:14-16 NLT)

As hard as I try, I cannot understand how people read these Scriptures yet still believe Jews remain a separate and distinct people of God apart from Christ? Please help me understand if the wall of separation came down with Christ (the veil was torn in two), why some Christian people want to put it back up by making a clear distinction between the two groups of people. I honestly can't tell if that is "adding to" or "taking away" from the Word of God.

> For by one Spirit we were <u>all baptized into one body—whether Jews or</u> <u>Greeks</u>, whether slaves or free—and have all been made to drink into[a] one Spirit.(1 Cor.12:13 NKJV)

How do proponents of "ethnic Israel" remaining a separate and distinct "people of God" reconcile this passage from Galatians?

> [22] The Scriptures say that Abraham had two sons, one from his slave wife and one from his freeborn wife.[a] [23] The son of the slave wife was born in a human attempt to bring about the fulfillment of God's promise. But <u>the son of</u> <u>the freeborn wife was born as God's own fulfillment of his promise.</u>

> [24] These two women serve as an illustration of God's two covenants. The first woman, Hagar, represents Mount Sinai where people received the law that enslaved them. [25] And <u>now Jerusalem</u> is just like Mount Sinai in Arabia,[b] because <u>she and her children live in slavery</u> to the law. [26] But the other woman, Sarah, represents the <u>heavenly Jerusalem.</u> She is the free woman, and <u>she is our mother.</u> [27] As Isaiah said,
> "Rejoice, O childless woman,
> you who have never given birth!
> Break into a joyful shout,
> you who have never been in labor!
> For the desolate woman now has more children
> than the woman who lives with her husband!"[c]

²⁸ And you, dear brothers and sisters, are children of the promise, just like Isaac. ²⁹ But you are now being persecuted by those who want you to keep the law, just as Ishmael, the child born by human effort, persecuted Isaac, the child born by the power of the Spirit.

³⁰ But what do the Scriptures say about that? "<u>Get rid of the slave and her son, for the son of the slave woman will not share the inheritance with the free woman's son.</u>"^[d] ³¹ So, dear brothers and sisters, we are not children of the slave woman; <u>we are children of the free woman.</u>   (Gal.4:22-32 NLT)

<u>Therefore know that only those who are of faith are sons of Abraham</u>. (Gal. 3:7 NKJV)

Faith in what? What else if not the Main Thing, "Jesus is THE CHRIST"

Jesus said to the Jews that "I know you are Abraham's descendants but you seek to kill Me because my word has no place in you" (John 8:37). The Jews answered Jesus and said to Him: <u>"Abraham is our father"</u> (John 8:39). In verse 41, the Jews told Jesus, "We have one father, God". The following passage was His answer:

Jesus told them, "If God were your Father, you would love me, because I have come to you from God. I am not here on my own, but he sent me. ⁴³ Why can't you understand what I am saying? It's because you can't even hear me! ⁴⁴ For <u>you are the children of your father the devil</u>, and you love to do the evil things he does. He was a murderer from the beginning. He has always hated the truth, because there is no truth in him. When he lies, it is consistent with his character; for he is a liar and the father of lies.
(John 8:42-44 NLT)

What this passage speaks to me is that those who actually have a connection to God the Father love and accept Jesus as the Christ. It seems that the reference Jesus is making is that the devil is the father of those who will not receive Him. I recently had someone tell me he believed this was just a reference to the resistive Jewish leadership of Jesus' day and not all the followers of Judaism throughout history continuing in the present day. Here again, one will have to decide for themselves, but I am unable to see what the differences might be to modern day opposition to Christ as "the Main Thing" and opposition in Old Testament days.

> *⁹ I know your affliction and distress and pressing trouble and your poverty—*
> *but you are rich! and how you are abused and reviled and slandered by those*
> *who <u>say they are Jews and are not, but are a synagogue of Satan.</u>*
> *(Rev.2:9 AMP)*

Again, do the words of Jesus just presented suggest there are people of God who are "real Jews" (God's chosen) and those who call themselves Jews but are imposters (not God's people)? Clearly Jesus is drawing a distinction to who is or is not a "real Jew".

The following surely maintains that there are two distinct and separate "descendants from Abraham", one group is said to be God's people and one group is NOT!

> *Well then, has God failed to fulfill his promise to Israel? No, for <u>not all who</u>*
> *<u>are born into the nation of Israel are truly members of God's people!</u> ² <u>Being</u>*
> *<u>descendants of Abraham doesn't make them truly Abraham's children.</u> For*
> *the Scriptures say, "Isaac is the son through whom your descendants will*
> *be counted,"[a] though Abraham had other children, too. ⁸ This means that*
> *<u>Abraham's physical descendants are not necessarily children of God.</u> Only the*
> *children of the promise are considered to be Abraham's children.*
> *(Rom.9:6-8 NLT)*

The Apostle Paul, an ethnic Jew himself, seems to understand and teach the difference.

> *A man is not a Jew just because he goes through the religious act of becoming a Jew. ²⁹ The true Jew is one whose heart is right with God. The religious act of becoming a Jew must be done in the heart. That is the work of the Holy Spirit. The Law does not do that kind of work. The true Jew gets his thanks from God, not from men (Rom. 2:28-29 NLV).*

The Old covenant has passed away, according to Hebrews, and a new people of God has been established.

> *It is not important if a man is circumcised or uncircumcised. The important thing is being the new people God has made. (Gal.6:15 NCV)*

This next verse is often used by advocates to argue for ethnic Israel but it is obviously tied to 6:15 as a continuation of the truth Paul is speaking that "those who walk after this rule" that God has created one "new people of God" are the "true" Israel of God.

> *Peace and mercy be upon all who walk by this rule [who discipline themselves and regulate their lives by this principle], even upon the [true] Israel of God! (Gal. 6:16 AMP)*

Just another example of the emphasis on the new creation:

> *If anyone belongs to Christ, there is a new creation. The old things have gone; everything is made new! (2 Cor. 5:17 NCV)*

And one more:

> *⁴⁷ Jesus saw Nathanael coming toward Him and said concerning him, See! Here is an Israelite indeed [a true descendant of Jacob], in whom there is no guile nor deceit nor falsehood nor duplicity! (John 1:47 AMP)*

I think you will agree that if you continue reading the above passage in your Bible, it plainly reveals in verse 49 what "rule" Nathanael, a "true Israelite" according to Jesus, decided to walk by.

The last Scripture makes it clear that all of those who will not listen to Jesus (receive His love and walk in it) will not ever be able to call themselves "God's people" because they have surely "cut themselves off from "God's people" through their rejection of Him! Remember that it was Moses speaking this to ethnic Israel in Deuteronomy 18:

> But God was fulfilling what _all the prophets_ had foretold about the Messiah—that he must suffer these things. *19* Now repent of your sins and turn to God, so that your sins may be wiped away. *20* Then times of refreshment will come from the presence of the Lord, and he will again send you Jesus, your appointed Messiah. *21* For he must remain in heaven until the time for the final restoration of all things, as God promised long ago through his holy prophets. *22* Moses said, 'The Lord your God will raise up for you a Prophet like me from among your own people. _Listen carefully to everything he tells you.'_ [a] *23* Then Moses said, '_Anyone who will not listen to that Prophet will be completely cut off from God's people. (Acts 3:18-23 NLT)_

The Main Thing

JESUS IS GOD

───❦───

When Jesus came to Caesarea Philippi, he asked his disciples, "Who are the people saying I am?"

14 "Well," they replied, "some say John the Baptist; some, Elijah; some, Jeremiah or one of the other prophets."

15 Then he asked them, "Who do you think I am?"

16 Simon Peter answered, "The Christ, the Messiah, the Son of the living God."(Matt.16:13-16 TLB)

Who do men say Jesus is/was today? Some say "just a man, a good man but still just a man". Some say He was a legend, He never really existed. Others say He was only a man and not a good one but was a liar. Still there are those who say He was only a man who was deranged and a lunatic.

Many of the world religions regard Him as a prophet, some say a great prophet but that is as far as it goes. Many say He was a created being, maybe a divine being but not God. Others think He was an archangel. Regardless, the rub with Jesus always comes down to "was He God or was He just a man".

The Christian faith is based on the fact that Jesus is God. If He was not God, how could His death have been sufficient to pay the penalty for our sins. If Jesus were not God He would be a created being and thus not qualified to pay the penalty required. Only God could take on the sins of the world, die and be resurrected, conquering sin and death on our behalf.

Published record that I have seen attests that 98% of professing Christians believe that Jesus is God. I cannot resist adding here as an aside that Jesus marveled at why people would be calling Him Lord (God) but yet would not obey His commands. Why would we say we believe He is God but not do what He said to do?

Regardless, the purpose of this segment is not to try to present all the historical evidence and logical reasoning that supports why Jesus was who "the Bible" affirms He was/is. I think it is very important for one to research that evidence because there is plenty out there to work through. I actually will make some recommendations about how I went about doing just that in a later chapter.

What I am interested in doing is presenting what Scripture reveals about Jesus, The Christ, who I am continuously heralding as "the Main Thing", being God. What the Bible is or is not, who Jesus is or is not, who or if there even is a God is all determined by faith. I made the statement earlier that faith is foremost to God. That which humans can prove beyond doubt with their natural minds and scientific conclusion is contradictory to the definition of faith. Faith is not even that easy to describe. The best I can do is: "firm persuasion, a conviction based upon hearing (as opposed to seeing). It is always used in the New Testament of faith in God or Christ, or things spiritual".

The Bible puts it this way:

> *Faith is the confidence that what we hope for will actually happen; it gives us assurance about <u>things we cannot see</u>. (Hebrews 11:1 NLT)*

So the point to this sector is to focus on what the Bible and Jesus say about Him (Jesus) in relation to the Godhead. We will assume that you either already now or may sometime in the future have "faith" that the Bible and what it says is the divinely inspired Word of God and thereby is the final authority for truth in the life of a Christian. I think that lack of clarity regarding "the divinity of Jesus" in relation to the Godhead is one of the major stumbling blocks in "Main Thing" consciousness.

Let's look to Scripture and see what it reveals about Jesus being God. I disclaim that I am including every passage relevant to this topic but rather those that are most compelling to me in my searching. I like to start in Isaiah:

> *Therefore the Lord Himself shall give you a sign: Behold, the young woman*
> *who is unmarried and a virgin shall conceive and bear a son,*
> *and shall call his name <u>Immanuel [God with us]</u>.*
> *(Isaiah 7:14 AMP)*

Really, we could stop right here and have our confirmation. Certainly, we are not going to do that. Immanuel is His name and Immanuel means GOD HIMSELF with us. Look what it says in Isaiah chapter nine about other names for Jesus:

> *For to us a Child is born, to us a Son is given; and the government shall*
> *be upon His shoulder, and His name shall be called Wonderful Counselor,*
> *<u>Mighty God, Everlasting Father [of Eternity]</u>, Prince of Peace.*
> *(Isaiah 9:6 AMP)*

I think it is more than just interesting that one of the names is Everlasting <u>FATHER</u>. Let's move on. The Word was God Himself and the Word (God) became flesh and lived among us.

*In the beginning [before all time] was the Word (Christ), and the Word was
with God, and <u>the Word was God Himself</u> (John 1:1 AMP)*

*<u>And the Word</u> (Christ) became flesh (human, incarnate) and tabernacled
(fixed His tent of flesh, lived awhile) among us; and we [actually] saw His
glory (His honor, His majesty), such glory as an only begotten son receives
from his father, full of grace (favor, loving-kindness) and truth.
(John 1:14 AMP)*

Well, that says a lot, but let's go on.

But we know that there is <u>only one God</u>, the Father, who created everything, and we live for him. And there is <u>only one Lord</u>, Jesus Christ, through
whom God made everything and through whom we have been given life.

Yes, ONE God and ONE Lord. But are they the same. Heed what Jesus said:

Philip said, "Lord, show us the Father and that will be enough for us."

*[9] Jesus answered: "Don't you know me, Philip, even after I have been among you such
a long time? <u>Anyone who has seen me has seen the Father.</u> How can you say, 'Show
us the Father'? [10] Don't you believe that <u>I am in the Father, and that the Father is
in me</u>? The words I say to you I do not speak on my own authority. Rather, it is <u>the
Father, living in me,</u> who is doing his work   (John 14:8-10 NIV)*

*<u>I give them eternal life</u>, and they will never perish. No one can snatch them away
from me, [29] for my Father has given them to me, and he is more powerful than anyone
else.] No one can snatch them from the Father's hand. <u>The Father and I are one.</u>"
(John 10:28-30 NLT)*

Who but God Himself can give eternal life? Then He says it plainly, "The
Father and I are one and the same. Here are a couple more confirmations
of the same exact message:

I will remain in the world no longer, but they are still in the world, and I am coming to you. Holy Father, protect them by the power of[a] your name, the name you gave me, so that they may be <u>one as we are one</u>.
(John 17:11 NIV)

That they all may be <u>one, [just] as You, Father, are in Me and I in You</u>, that they also may be <u>one in Us</u>, so that the world may believe and be convinced that You have sent Me. (John 17:21 AMP)

The Apostle Paul acknowledges the same oneness:

Your attitude should be the kind that was shown us by Jesus Christ, ⁶ who, <u>though he was God</u>, did not demand and cling to his rights as God, (Philippians 2:5-6 TLB)

Paul again, this time to the Corinthians:

Satan, who is the god of this world, has blinded the minds of those who don't believe. They are unable to see the glorious light of the Good News. They don't understand this message about the glory of <u>Christ, who is the exact likeness of God. (2 Cor.4:4</u> NLT)

In Hebrews, referring to a passage in Psalm 45 has God calling Jesus God. How about that for authentication?

but <u>of his Son</u> he says, "<u>Your Kingdom, O God</u>, will last forever and ever; its commands are always just and right. ⁹ You love right and hate wrong; so God, even your God, has poured out more gladness upon you than on anyone else."(Hebrews 1:8-9 TLB)

Who created the heavens and the earth according to the Old Testament?

In the beginning <u>God</u> created the heaven and the earth. (Gen. 1:1 KJV)

Who created the heavens and the earth according to the New Testament?

> *[Now] He is the [a]<u>exact likeness of the unseen</u> <u>God</u> [the visible*
> *representation of the invisible]; He is the*
> *Firstborn of all creation.*
>
> *[16] For it was <u>in Him that all things were created, in heaven and on earth</u>,*
> *things seen and things unseen, whether thrones, dominions, rulers, or*
> *authorities<u>; all things were created and exist through Him</u> [by His service,*
> *intervention] and in and for Him.*
>
> *[17] And He Himself existed before all things, and <u>in Him all things consist</u>*
> *(cohere, are held together). (Col.1:15-17 AMP)*

I feel it safe to say that either the Bible is contradicting itself or Jesus Christ and the God of the Old Testament are one and the same.

That is straight forward enough. Let's look back to the Old Testament for a moment:

> *Do we not all have one Father[a]? <u>Did not one God create us</u>? Why do we*
> *profane the covenant of our ancestors by being unfaithful to one another?*
> *(Malachi 2:10 NIV)*

One God, not two created us! Once again, Jesus is just God who took on a human body.

> *For in Christ there is <u>all of God</u> in a human body; (Col. 2:9 TLB)*

> Now back to the Old Testament again for more. Remember the burning
> bush story between God and Moses?

But Moses protested, "If I go to the people of Israel and tell them, 'The God of your ancestors has sent me to you,' they will ask me, 'What is his name?' Then what should I tell them?"

[14] God replied to Moses, <u>"I AM WHO I AM.</u>[a] Say this to the people of Israel: <u>I AM</u> has sent me to you." [15] God also said to Moses, "Say this to the people of Israel: Yahweh,[b] <u>the God of your ancestors—the God of Abraham, the God of Isaac, and the God of Jacob</u>—has sent me to you.

*This is my eternal name,
<u>my name to remember for all generations. (Ex.3:13-15 NLT)</u>*

The God of the Old Testament, the God of Abraham, Isaac and Jacob, Yahweh told Moses His eternal name for all generations is <u>"I AM"</u>.

Now to the New Testament again for the words of Jesus:

The people said, "You aren't even fifty years old. How can you say you have seen Abraham?

[58] Jesus answered, "I tell you the truth, before <u>Abraham</u> was even born, <u>I AM!</u>"(John 8:37-58 NLT)

Consider these passages where Jesus uses I AM:

John 6:51:<u>"I AM</u> the living bread which came down from heaven. If anyone eats of this bread, he will live forever;"

John 8:23: And He said to them, "You are from beneath; <u>I AM</u> from above. You are of this world; I am not of this world.

John 8:12: Then Jesus spoke to them again, saying, "<u>I AM</u> the light of the world. He who follows Me shall not walk in darkness, but have the light of life."

John 8:58 Jesus said to them, "Most assuredly, I say to you, before Abraham was, <u>I AM</u>."

John 10:9: "<u>I AM</u> the door. If anyone enters by Me, he will be saved, and will go in and out and find pasture."

John 10:11: "<u>I AM</u> the good shepherd. The good shepherd gives His life for the sheep.

John 10:36: "do you say of Him whom the Father sanctified and sent into the world, 'You are blaspheming,' because I said, '<u>I AM</u> the Son of God'?

John 11:25: Jesus said to her, "<u>I AM</u> the resurrection and the life. He who believes in Me, though he may die, he shall live.

John 14:6: Jesus said to him, "<u>I AM</u> the way, the truth, and the life. No one comes to the Father except through Me.

John 15:1: "<u>I AM</u> the true vine, and My Father is the vinedresser.

John 19:2: Therefore the chief priests of the Jews said to Pilate, "Do not write, 'The King of the Jews,' but, 'He said, "<u>I AM</u> the King of the Jews."'"

Acts 7:32: Stephen speaking of Moses' encounter at the burning bush "saying, '<u>I AM</u> the God of your fathers-- the God of Abraham, the God of Isaac, and the God of Jacob.' And Moses trembled and dared not look."

Acts 9:5: And he said, "Who are You, Lord?" And the Lord said, "<u>I AM</u> Jesus, whom you are persecuting. It is hard for you to kick against the goads."

Yes He is our GREAT GOD and our blessed SAVIOR:

> *while we wait for the blessed hope—the appearing of the glory of <u>our great</u>*
> *<u>God and Savior, Jesus Christ</u>‡ who gave himself for us to redeem us from all*
> *wickedness and to purify for himself a people that are his very own,*
> *eager to do what is good. (Titus 2:13-14 NIV)*

Who but God knows men's hearts?

> *Then hear in heaven, Your dwelling place, and forgive and act and give*
> *to every man according to his ways, whose heart You know, <u>for You and</u>*
> *<u>You only</u> know the hearts of all the children of men,*
> *(1 Kings 8:39 AMP)*

Only God knows the hearts of men. See what Jesus said of Himself relevant to this issue:

> *I will strike her children dead. Then all the churches will know that <u>I am he</u>*
> *<u>who searches hearts and minds</u>, and I will repay each of you*
> *according to your deeds (Rev. 2:23 NIV)*

Who but God alone is to be worshipped? Consider these passages, the first from the Old Testament and the second from Jesus as He was addressing the devil in the wilderness.

> *Respect the LORD your God. You <u>must worship him</u> and make your*
> *promises <u>only in his name</u>. (Deut.6:13 NCV)*

> *"Get out of here, Satan," Jesus told him. "The Scriptures say, '<u>Worship only</u>*
> *<u>the Lord God</u>. Obey only him." (Matt. 4:10 TLB)*

Only God is to be worshipped but Jesus received worship recurrently.

And when they were come into the house, they saw the young child with Mary his mother, and fell down, and <u>worshipped him</u>: and when they had opened their treasures, they presented unto him gifts; gold, and frankincense and myrrh. (Matt 2:11 KJV)

Then came she <u>and worshipped him</u>, saying, Lord, help me. (Matt.15:25 KJV)

And, behold, there came a leper <u>and worshipped him</u>, saying, Lord, if thou wilt, thou canst make me clean. (Matt.8:2 KJV)

And as they went to tell his disciples, behold, Jesus met them, saying, All hail. And they came and held him by the feet, <u>and worshipped him</u>. (Matt.28:9 KJV)

And when they saw him, <u>they worshipped him</u>: but some doubted. (Matt. 28:17 KJV)

Only God can forgive sins, right.

<u>I, even I, am He Who blots out and cancels your transgressions,</u> for My own sake, and I will not remember your sins. (Isaiah 43:25 AMP)

Even the unbelieving Jews knew this!

Why does this [a]Man talk like this? He is blaspheming! <u>Who can forgive sins</u> [[b]remove guilt, remit the penalty, and bestow righteousness instead] <u>except God alone?</u>(Mark 2:7 AMP)

Well, Jesus forgave sins, didn't He?

Is it easier to say 'Your sins are forgiven,' or 'Stand up and walk'? [6] So I will prove to you that <u>the Son of Man[a] has the authority on earth to forgive</u>

sins." Then Jesus turned to the paralyzed man and said, "Stand up, pick up your mat, and go home!"(Matt. 9:56 NLT)

Okay, let's do one more thing here. Let's go to Revelation and look at a few verses there and see what happens.

From: John To: The seven churches in Turkey.[a]Dear Friends:

May you have grace and peace from God who is, and was, and is to come; and from the sevenfold Spirit* before his throne;⁵ and from Jesus Christ who faithfully reveals all truth to us. He was the first to rise from death, to die no more.[b] He is far greater than any king in all the earth. All praise to him who always loves us and who set us free from our sins by pouring out his lifeblood for us. (Rev.1:4-5 TLB)

So if we were to stop right here, it looks to me like God "who is, was, and is to come" is depicted as somehow separate from Jesus Christ, wouldn't you agree. But let's keep going a little farther. Jesus makes a very strong and interesting declaration just a few verses later:

I am the Alpha and the Omega, the Beginning and the End, says the Lord God, He Who is and Who was and Who is to come, the Almighty (the Ruler of all). (Rev.1:8 AMP)

Now when I first saw this, I did several double takes before it really settled in. Clearly, in verse 4 it is speaking of God as though He was distinct from Jesus because He (God) was referred to as "He who is, was and is to come". In verse 8 it is clearly Jesus saying it is He "who is, was and is to come. This description of God is repeated in Chapter 4:8 but something interesting happens before we get that far:

After this I looked, and behold, a door standing open in heaven! And the first voice which I had heard addressing me like [the calling of] a [a]war trumpet said, Come up here, and I will show you what must take place in the future.

At once I came under the [Holy] Spirit's power, and behold, <u>a throne stood in heaven,</u>
<u>with One</u> seated on the throne! (Rev.4:1-2 AMP)

Did you see that? There is only <u>ONE</u> sitting on the throne! Who is the
<u>ONE</u> on the throne? Let's go back to Chapter 4 verse 8:

And the four living creatures, individually having six wings, were full of eyes
all over and within [underneath their wings]; and day and night they never
stop saying, Holy, holy, holy is the Lord God Almighty (Omnipotent), <u>Who</u>
<u>was and Who is and Who is to come (Rev.4:8 AMP)</u>

Chapter 4 ends with verse 11 making it even more clear who it is on the
throne. Not only do we see the <u>"is, was, and is to come"</u> business again
but we see that the <u>ONE</u> who is being worshipped is the <u>ONE</u> who created the heavens and the earth. I believe we have already established the
creator was Jesus(The Word of God).

Worthy are You, our Lord and God, to receive the glory and the honor and
dominion, for <u>You created all things; by Your will they were [brought into</u>
<u>being] and were created.</u> (Rev.4:11 AMP)

Progressing along to Chapter 6, we see more collaboration:

And they called to the mountains and the rocks, Fall on (before) us and hide
us from the face of <u>Him Who sits on the throne</u> and from the [a]deep-seated
indignation and wrath of <u>the Lamb.</u>

[17] For the great day of His wrath (vengeance, retribution, indignation) has
come, and who is able to stand before (Rev.6:16-17 AMP)

Let's look next at Chapter 7:

After the vision of these things I looked, and there was a great number of
people, so many that no one could count them. They were from every nation,
tribe, people, and language of the earth. They were all standing before <u>the</u>

*throne and before the Lamb, wearing white robes and holding palm branches
in their hands. ^{10} They were shouting in a loud voice, "Salvation belongs to
our God, who sits on the throne, and to the Lamb." (Rev.7:9-10 NCV)*

Whether we be good scholars or not, most of us understand that the
Lamb is definitely Jesus, "The Main Thing" and that there is ONE on
the throne. Again it sounds like two but they must be one and the same.
Isn't that what Jesus was saying so profusely in the book of John. "I and
the Father are one. If you have seen Me you have seen the Father".

Revelation chapter 21 begins with John witnessing a new heaven and a new
earth that is replacing the old ones that have passed away. The vision is punc-
tuated by the Holy city, the NEW Jerusalem descending out of heaven. It is
here in this city that God finally climaxes His plan that has been in place from
the beginning, "to have a people for Himself" and to be with them forever.
Those whose names are written in the Lamb's Book of Life will be His people
and He will be their God. The city has no temple in it because the Lord God
Almighty and the Lamb **are** its temple. Now back to the throne:

*Then he showed me the river whose waters give life, sparkling like crystal,
flowing out from the throne of God and of the Lamb*

*^{2} Through the middle of the broadway of the city; also, on either side of the
river was the tree of life with its twelve varieties of fruit, yielding each month
its fresh crop; and the leaves of the tree were for the healing and the restoration
of the nations.*

*^{3} There shall no longer exist there anything that is accursed (detestable, foul,
offensive, impure, hateful, or horrible). But the throne of God and of the
Lamb shall be in it, and His servants shall worship Him [pay divine honors
to Him and do Him holy service].*

*^{4} They shall see His face, and His name shall be on their foreheads.
(Rev.22:1-4 AMP)*

Could we have a misprint here or have we finally found an error in the Bible. I don't think so. The throne is occupied by "God **and** the Lamb" but very clearly the throne dweller is referenced in the singular person, HIS and HIM.

Without a doubt, God Almighty and Jesus Christ are one and the same.

How does Almighty God end the Bible, His story:

> *Behold, I AM coming soon, and I shall bring My wages and rewards with Me, to repay and render to each one just what his own actions and his own work merit.*
>
> *¹³ I am the Alpha and the Omega, the First and the Last (the Before all and the End of all (Rev. 22:12-13 AMP)*

Jesus Christ, God almighty, the Lamb, the Alpha and Omega, the Before all and the End of all is unmistakably "the ONE True God"—not just "The Main Thing" but "The EVERYTHING".

He says He is coming for us "quickly" and He expects us to be watching for Him.

Is there really anything more important in our walk with God than to be focusing all of our attention on Him personally and relationally so He will recognize and claim us when He comes??

GOD'S ROYAL LAW

———— ᙨᙠᙦ ————

Sir Isaac Newton was an English physicist and mathematician who lived in the 1600's. He is still regarded by many as the most famous scientist who has ever lived. You may remember from school that he is the one we see sitting under the fruit tree with a falling apple about to bang him on the head. Among many other principles, he discovered gravity and it became known as "Newton's Law". There are many other "laws" that bear his name and are referred to as "Newton's Law of (fill in the blank). All those laws are a reflection of the heart of who Newton really was, a great scientist.

Doesn't it just make sense that "God's Law" would also be a reflection of His heart, of Who He really is?

I have seen several sources that indicate "law" is not that easy to label. The following definition was taken from the dictionary.com website and gives a secular description of the word "law":

law

1. the principles and regulations established in a <u>community</u> by some authority and applicable to its people, whether in the form of legislation or of custom and policies recognized and enforced by judicial <u>decision</u>.

2. any written or positive rule or collection of rules prescribed under the authority of the state or nation, as by the people in its <u>constitution</u>. Compare <u>bylaw</u>, <u>statute law</u>.

3. the controlling influence of such rules; the condition of society brought about by their observance: *maintaining law and order.*

4. a system or collection of such rules.

5. the department of knowledge concerned with these rules; jurisprudence: *to study law.*

In English we generally understand "law" to mean regulations or statutes instituted by some governing power that must be obeyed or else we will be in trouble. In this sense, when laws are broken, punishment is imposed. I think that sadly, many people view God in this perspective. They erringly suppose that He has put forth this set of "commandments" for the sole purpose of heaping eternal damnation upon those who will not "toe the line" and obey His strict decrees.

But does this same definition apply to God's law? In the Bible, the Hebrew word for law is **torah.** It means "direction, teaching, instruction". God's law then is a little different than man's law, would you agree? His law is more for teaching, directing and instructing us how we should choose to live than just to beat us if we get out of line.

> *My son, do not forget <u>my law,</u>*
> *But let your heart <u>keep my commands;</u>*
> *For length of days and long life*
> *And peace they will add to you.*
> *Let not mercy and truth forsake you;*
> *Bind them around your neck,*
> *<u>Write them on the tablet of your heart,</u>*

And so find favor and high esteem
In the sight of God and man.
Trust in the LORD with all your heart,
And lean not on your own understanding; (Proverbs 3:1-5 NKJ)

It appears to me that the sole purpose of God's law is to teach mankind the way to find the "life" that He wants His kids to have. He tells us that we will find that life if we will "write His law on the tablet of our heart and trust Him instead of our own understanding" Why does He tell us that? Again, He emphasizes that is how we find the "life" He has for us to live!

My child, pay attention to what I say.
Listen carefully to my words.¹ Don't lose sight of them.
Let them penetrate deep into your heart,²for they bring life
to those who find them,
and healing to their whole body.³ Guard your heart above all else,
for it determines the course of your life
(Proverbs 4:20-23 NLT)

His laws and commands are for our benefit, not condemnation. Most good parents have rules and guidelines for their children to obey and follow. Don't play in the highway because you could get run over by a car. Don't hang out in dreadful places with the wrong type of people because nothing good for you can come from it. Be home by midnight because more evil things are going on at that hour than good things. We are concerned for our children's welfare so we set boundaries for them to follow for their own good, not so we can lord over them just because we have the authority. We believe that if our children will follow the rules their life will be much better than if they refuse.

It is no different with God. As guardians for our children, we are supposed to be getting the rules and regulations we set for our family to follow from Him because He is the perfect parent. Isn't that why He wants us to call Him Father?

I have said all that to say this: "I have come to believe that God's law is just God's love". I can't exactly prove that with direct Scripture references but I think we can look at passages that when examined from a "Main Thing" perspective can definitely lead to that conclusion. Let's take a look at how God's love and God's law seem to coincide throughout the Bible.

Many people believe and teach today that Godly love is taught only in the New Testament. I believe that is incorrect. I have exhaustively attempted to convey in this entire work how that Jesus Christ is "the entirety of all Scripture". Jesus Christ and God are One and the same and God IS love. Ergo, Jesus IS love. Love IS the centerpiece of both the Old and the New Testaments.

It is in the Old Testament where we first find the "law" of loving our neighbor as ourselves:

> Forget about the wrong things people do to you, and do not try to get even. <u>Love your neighbor as you love yourself</u>. I am the LORD. (Lev.19:18 NCV)

Many people today identify God's law only with the commandments given through Moses at Sinai. I think Scripture reveals that God's law was in effect long before the Ten Commandments were written on stone. Consider the proof in the following article:

Did the Ten Commandments Exist Before Moses?

"Many people assume that the Ten Commandments and the covenant God established with ancient Israel are identical—and that both were abolished by Jesus Christ's death. They believe that the Sinai Covenant and God's commandments came into existence together and went out of existence together.

But is such reasoning biblical? The facts show *it is not*. A close look at the Scriptures reveals that breaking the Ten Commandments was a sin before the covenant at Mt. Sinai, so arguments that they came into existence with that covenant and were terminated with it cannot be true. Let's notice the scriptural proof.

God's Word defines **sin** as "the transgression of the law" (1 John 3:4, KJV) or "lawlessness" (New King James Version, NIV). Therefore, "where there is no law there is no transgression" (Romans 4:15). This is what the Bible clearly says! So do we find transgressions of the Ten Commandments described as sinful before Mt. Sinai? Clearly we do.

For example, Genesis 13:13 tells us that "the men of Sodom were *exceedingly wicked and sinful* against the Lord." Since sin is violating God's law, the people of Sodom could not have been punished for being wicked and sinful if no law condemned what they were doing. We must conclude, therefore, that God had already made available the knowledge of what is sinful.

Here is a clear example. Genesis 20:3-9 and 39:7-9 describe adultery as "a great sin" and a "sin against God." Adultery breaks the *Seventh Commandment*.

In Genesis 3:6 and 17, God punishes Adam and Eve for their coveting and stealing—breaking the *Tenth and Eighth Commandments*. They also dishonored Him as their parent, violating the *Fifth Commandment*.

In Genesis 4:9-12, God punishes Cain for murder and lying—violations of the *Sixth and Ninth Commandments*.

In Exodus 16:4, several days to several weeks before God established His covenant with the Israelites at Mt. Sinai, we find God giving them a test to see "whether they will walk in My law or not." His test involved whether they would rest on the seventh-day Sabbath as He commanded in the *Fourth Commandment* of that law—with which they were at least partly familiar. The seventh day had been hallowed—set aside as holy by God—from the time of Adam and Eve (Genesis 2:1-3).

God's reaction to their disobedience is revealing. He exclaims, "How long do you refuse to keep *My commandments and My laws?*" (Exodus 16: 28). God clearly speaks of both His "commandments and . . . laws" as <u>already existing and in force well before He listed the Ten Commandments verbally at Mt. Sinai</u>, as described four chapters later! Therefore, the Ten Commandments were only *codified*—<u>written in stone as part of a formal covenant</u>—at Mt. Sinai. Scripture clearly shows that they existed and were in force well before then.

This is stated explicitly in Genesis 26:5, where God tells Isaac that He blessed his father Abraham "because *Abraham <u>obeyed</u> My voice and <u>kept</u> My charge, My commandments, My statutes, and <u>My laws</u>.*" This event took place centuries before the covenant at Mt. Sinai, centuries before Moses and two generations before Judah, head of the tribe that much later would become known as the Jews, was born! (Be sure to read "Did Abraham Keep the Same Commandments God Gave to Moses?" on page 13).

In Leviticus 18:21 and 27, God calls the idolatrous practices of the people of the land of Canaan "abominations"—actions so filthy and degrading that God compared their expulsion to being "vomited out" of the land (verse 28). What was their sin? Among other things, idolatry (the worship of false gods) and human sacrifice, which violated the *First, Second* and *Sixth Commandments.*

The Bible shows that the Ten Commandments did not originate with Moses or in his time. Nor were they in any way limited only to the Jews. They were in effect and known long before Moses or a people known as the Jews existed. <u>They are the foundation of God's laws that show us how to love God (defined by the first four Commandments) and how to love our fellow man (defined by the last six).</u>" 1

Is there any evidence at all that God's law of love was operational way back in the beginning. I think there is a strong possibility. I think the biblical account of Cain and Abel reveals enough for us to make calculated suppositions pertaining to our subject matter at hand. You know the story. Adam and Eve have two sons. Cain is the oldest and Abel is the younger. Cain was a farmer and Abel raised livestock. In time, The Bible says, both men brought offerings to the Lord. The Lord received Abel's offering but refused to accept Cain's. Cain's selfish anger boiled over and he killed his brother. Let's look at the passage and then come back to some comments:

And Adam knew Eve as his wife, and she became pregnant and bore Cain; and she said, I have gotten and gained a man with the help of the Lord.

and [next] she gave birth to his brother Abel. Now Abel was a keeper of sheep, but Cain was a tiller of the ground.

³ And in the course of time Cain brought to the Lord an offering of the fruit of the ground.

And Abel brought of the firstborn of his flock and of the fat portions. And the Lord had respect and regard for Abel and for his offering,

But for [a] Cain and his offering He had no respect or regard. So Cain was exceedingly angry and indignant, and he looked sad and depressed.

And the Lord said to Cain, Why are you angry? And why do you look sad and depressed and dejected?

If you do well, will you not be accepted? And if you do not do well, sin crouches at your door; its desire is for you, but you must master it.

And Cain said to his brother, [b] Let us go out to the field. And when they were in the field, Cain rose up against Abel his brother and killed him.

And the Lord said to Cain, Where is Abel your brother? And he said, I do not know. Am I my brother's keeper?

And [the Lord] said, What have you done? The voice of your brother's blood is crying to Me from the ground.

And now you are cursed by reason of the earth, which has opened its mouth to receive your brother's [shed] blood from your hand. (Gen.4:1-11 AMP)

Let's start unpacking what we have heard in this story and see what we can identify. The article we read established from Scripture that "sin is transgression of the law" and where there is no law there is no transgression". God Himself told Cain that sin was present so there had to be laws of some kind in affect. The article also noted that God punishes Cain (actually Cain brings the judgment on himself for violating the law) for murder and lying—violations of the Sixth and Ninth Commandments.

We also know for truth that the greatest of all the Commandments, the laws that "all the law and the Prophets" depend on are to "love God with all your heart" and to love your neighbor (brother in this case) as you love yourself". We have also determined that God is no respecter of persons, but we know He received Abel's offering but rejected Cain's. I have heard a lot of speculation of why God acted in this manner but never any explanation that makes more sense than what I am about to propose. Let me share another passage from the New Testament where Jesus is defining "murder" under the new covenant:

"You have heard that it was said to our people long ago, 'You must not murder anyone.[a] Anyone who murders another will be judged.' But I tell you, if you are angry with a brother or sister,[b] you will be judged. If you say bad things to a brother or sister, you will be judged by the council. And if you call someone a fool, you will be in danger of the fire of hell.

"So when you offer your gift to God at the altar, and you remember that your brother or sister has something against you, leave your gift there at the

altar. Go and make peace with that person, <u>and then come and offer your gift.</u>
(Matt. 5:21-24 NCV)

I believe that it is more probable than likely that the reason God refused to accept Cain's offering was because Cain was violating God's requirements of love and reverence for Him and for his brother Abel. It seems logical that this disrespect had been taking place for a long time. I can easily see how God might have been saying to Cain all along that he needed to go make peace with his brother Abel and then bring your gift back and I will accept it. When Cain answers God with a lie, "I don't have any idea where my brother is", that shows me that he had a lack of reverence for God. That is further backed up with his smart aleck remark, "Am I my brother's keeper"? Who talks to God that way? I think it is highly likely that Cain knew full well that God's law required him to be "his brother's keeper" and he chose not to "do what was right" before God.

Last note on this scenario. God told Cain that if he would "do right" things would go well for him and he was capable of "ruling over" the "sin" that would ultimately lead him away from God. He refused to listen and garnished severe punishment in return.

> *So now we can tell who are children of God and who are children of the devil.*
> *Anyone who does not live righteously and <u>does not love other believers^[a] does</u>*
> <u>*not belong to God*</u> *¹ This is the message you have heard from the beginning:*
> <u>*We should love one another.*</u> *² We must not be like Cain, who belonged to the*
> *evil one and killed his brother. And why did he kill him? Because <u>Cain had</u>*
> <u>*been doing what was evil, and his brother had been doing what was righteous.*</u>
> *(1 John 3:10-12 NLT)*

Please see this. Cain brought the curse upon himself through disobedience and disrespect for God's law of love as opposed to God punishing him for his daring to rebel against a set of rules and regulations.

I believe that God's commandments to love Him and to love each other was in place at creation and has carried through the ages to the present !

So we have made the strong case from the Old Testament that God's law was in place long before the Ten Commandments were given to Israel at Mt. Sinai. Let's go now to see what we can find in the New Testament relative to this issue.

Can the law of love be tied specifically to the Ten Commandments? See what you think:

> *Yes indeed, it is good when you obey <u>the royal law</u> as found in the Scriptures: "<u>Love your neighbor as yourself.</u>"[a] But if you favor some people over others, you are committing a sin. You are guilty of breaking the law.[0] For the person who keeps all of the laws except one is as guilty as a person who has broken all of God's laws[1] For the same God who said, "You must not commit adultery," also said, "You must not murder."[b] So if you murder someone but do not commit adultery, you have still broken the law.(James 2:8-11 NLT)*

The "royal" law, the sovereign decree of a King is "love your neighbor as yourself" and is definitely connected to the Ten Commandments in this passage from James.

Love really is the summation of the Ten Commandments according to Paul:

> *Let no debt remain outstanding, except the continuing debt to <u>love one another, for whoever loves others has fulfilled the law. The commandments.</u> "You shall not commit adultery," "You shall not murder," "You shall not steal," "You shall not covet,"[a] and whatever other command there may be, <u>are summed up</u> in this one command: "<u>Love your neighbor as yourself.</u>" Love*

does no harm to a neighbor. Therefore love is the fulfillment of the law.
(Romans 13:8-10 NIV)

The question that comes to my mind is: "If loving God and one another
is not the totality of God's law, how could God's law be summed up and
fulfilled by loving alone? If the law has any other component than love,
wouldn't that other component be left out?"

We know what Jesus has said about the Commandments:

but not the Pharisees! When they heard that he had routed the Sadducees
with his reply, they thought up a fresh question of their own to ask him. One
of them, a lawyer, spoke up: "Sir, which is the most important
command in the laws of Moses?"

Jesus replied, "'Love the Lord your God with all your heart, soul,
and mind.' This is the first and greatest commandment. The second
most important is similar: 'Love your neighbor as much as you love
yourself.' 40 All the other commandments and all the demands of
the prophets stem from these two laws and are fulfilled if you obey
them. Keep only these and you will find that you are obeying all the
others."(Matt.22:35-40 TLB)

Jesus said His purpose was to fulfill the "royal" law of God that sinful
man is not capable of keeping in and of himself.

"Don't think that I have come to destroy the law of Moses or the teaching of the
prophets. I have not come to destroy them but to bring about what they said. (Matt.
5:17 NCV)

For Christ has already accomplished the purpose for which the law was given.[a] As a
result, all who believe in him are made right with God. (Rom. 10:4 NLT)

Recall what He told us about how that purpose was accomplished:

The greatest love a person can show is to die for his friends. (John 15:13 NCV)

Stated again in 1 John:

We know what <u>real love is from Christ's example</u> in dying for us. And so we also ought to lay down our lives for our Christian brothers. (1 John 3:16 TLB)

So here's the deal. God's law is perfect love. The law was codified in the Ten Commandments to reveal our sin and show us the only way we would ever satisfy the holiness that God requires is in Christ. There never has been an expectation that man could keep the codified law and any attempts to try and do so are futile and demonstrate our lack of understanding of the law. Any form of legalism can cause us to wittingly or unwittingly "trample on the Son of God" and "count the blood of the covenant which has sanctified us as a common thing".

How much division, dissention and fighting go on over debates about law keeping? The Apostle Paul told the Galatians that we should be serving one another in love thereby satisfying God's standard for us. Please note what he said would happen if we choose to bite and devour one another-----<u>We will destroy each other!</u>

You, my brothers and sisters, were called to be free. But do not use your freedom to indulge the flesh[a]; rather, <u>serve one another humbly in love.</u> [14] For <u>the entire law is fulfilled in keeping this one command: "Love your neighbor as yourself.</u> If you bite and devour each other, <u>watch out or you will be destroyed by each other.</u>
(Gal. 5:13-15 NIV)

So let's go back to where we started in this segment. We presented two passages from Proverbs where God appeals to man to "write His law (commands) on the tablet of your heart" and let His law penetrate deep into your heart" because it is His law that brings the "life". He was saying, "You do it as an act of your will". I want you to freely choose to love Me and to love your neighbor as you love yourself". That was under the old covenant God made with Israel.

At another point in time God says, "I am going to PUT my law in their heart. I will do the writing on the tablet of their hearts Myself".

"Behold, the days are coming, says the LORD, when I will make a new covenant with the house of Israel and with the house of Judah² not according to the covenant that I made with their fathers in the day that I took them by the hand to lead them out of the land of Egypt, My covenant which they broke, though I was a husband to them,[a]*says the LORD.³ But this is the covenant that I will make with the house of Israel after those days, says the LORD: I will put My law in their minds, and write it on their hearts; and I will be their God, and they shall be My people. No more shall every man teach his neighbor, and every man his brother, saying, 'Know the LORD,' for they all shall know Me, from the least of them to the greatest of them, says the LORD. For I will forgive their iniquity, and their sin I will remember no more." (Jeremiah 31:31-34 NKJ)*

Clearly, life as God wants us to have is found when His law "is written on our hearts"?

How is God's law written on our hearts?

Clearly, you are a letter from Christ showing the result of our ministry among you. This "letter" is written not with pen and ink, but with the Spirit of the living God. It is carved not on tablets of stone, but on human hearts ⁴ We are confident of all this because of our great trust in God through Christ ⁵ It is not that we think we are qualified to do anything on our own. Our qualification comes from God. ⁶ He has enabled us to be ministers of his new covenant. This is a covenant not of written laws, but of the Spirit. The old written covenant ends in death; but under the new covenant, the Spirit gives life.
(2 Corinthians 3:3-6 NLT)

It is the "Spirit" that gives life. Where do we get the Spirit that gives life"?

> *So now there is no condemnation for <u>those who belong to Christ Jesus. And</u>*
> *<u>because you belong to him,</u> the power[a] of the life-giving Spirit has freed*
> *you[b] from the power of sin that leads to death.[3] The law of Moses was unable*
> *to save us because of the weakness of our sinful nature.[c] So <u>God did what the</u>*
> *<u>law could not do</u>. He sent his own Son in a body like the bodies we sinners*
> *have. And in that body God declared an end to sin's control over us by giving*
> *his Son as a sacrifice for our sins. He did this so that <u>the just requirement of</u>*
> *<u>the law would be fully satisfied for us,</u> who no longer follow our sinful nature*
> *but instead follow the Spirit. (Rom. 8:1-4 NLT)*

We get the Spirit by BELONGING to Christ. The Law of Moses could not save us because the whole world (all mankind) was in bondage to sin. The just requirement of the law (love God and each other) could only be satisfied by One who was not bound by sin. That role had to be filled by One who was fully human and fully God at the same time. Certainly, we know that person is Jesus Christ (God Himself in the form of a man) who was called The Son of God. The purpose of the codified law was to bring us to Christ! It never had the ability or purpose to save us. The law was not capable of making us right with God!

The Purpose of the Law of Moses

[1] Does this mean that the law is against God's promises? Never! That would be true only if the law could make us right with God. <u>But God did not give a law that can bring</u> <u>life.</u> Instead, the Scriptures showed that the whole world is bound by sin. This was so the promise would be given through faith to people who believe in Jesus Christ.

> *Before this faith came, we were <u>all held prisoners by the law</u>. We had no*
> *freedom until God showed us the way of faith that was coming. In other*
> *words, <u>the law was our guardian leading us to Christ so that we could be</u>*
> *<u>made right with God through faith.</u> Now the way of faith has come, and we*
> *<u>no longer live under a guardian</u>.*

You were all baptized into Christ, and so you were all clothed with Christ.
This means that you are all children of God through faith in Christ Jesus.
(Gal.3:21-27 NCV)

We **belong** to Christ and become God's children the same way Abraham qualified—by believing in Him. "Only those of faith are sons of Abraham" (Gal.3:7). Attempting to keep any part of the Law under the old covenant after Christ came is to completely miss the sole purpose of why He had to come and do what He did to rescue us.

> *For Christ is the end of the Law [the limit at which it ceases to be, for the Law leads up to Him Who is the fulfillment of its types, and in Him the purpose which it was designed to accomplish is fulfilled. That is, the purpose of the Law is fulfilled in Him] as the means of righteousness (right relationship to God) for everyone who trusts in and adheres to and relies on Him. (Rom. 10:4 AMP).*

After Christ has come, there must be something required of us to keep our part of the "new covenant". There is. We must BELONG to Him through faith. How is that accomplished and how can we be sure we "know" Him which is the way to have eternal life (John 17:3)?

> *And we can be sure that we know him if we obey his commandments.⁴ If someone claims, "I know God," but doesn't obey God's commandments, that person is a liar and is not living in the truth. But those who obey God's word truly show how completely they love him. That is how we know we are living in him. (1 John 2:3-5 NLT)*

What has Jesus told us that we need to do to belong to Him? Well, to begin with let's remember that Jesus said that all the law hangs on two commandments, "love your God with all your heart and love your neighbor as yourself". We have previously offered that God's law was just the essence of who He was, is and always will be. We are not able to satisfy that law in and of ourselves but we can keep the law of love by "abiding" in Him and that free will choice gives us the power to be like Him (love unconditionally) and His love changes our hearts.

Loving One Another

*7 Dear friends, let us continue to love one another, for love comes from God. Anyone who loves is a child of God and knows God. 8 But anyone who does not love does not know God, **for God is love.***

9 God showed how much he loved us by sending his one and only Son into the world so that we might have eternal life through him. 10 This is real love—not that we loved God, but that he loved us and sent his Son as a sacrifice to take away our sins.

11 Dear friends, since God loved us that much, we surely ought to love each other. 12 No one has ever seen God. But if we love each other, God lives in us, and his love is brought to full expression in us.

13 And God has given us his Spirit as proof that we live in him and he in us.(1John 4:7-13 NLT)

We were not and are not capable of keeping God's law (loving like He loves) in and of ourselves. We are only able to achieve the righteousness God requires of us through the love He has in Himself that we access by "abiding" (dwelling) in Christ. Please consider how Jesus expresses this truth through John:

I am the True Vine, and My Father is the Vinedresser.

2 Any branch in Me that does not bear fruit [that stops bearing] He cuts away (trims off, takes away); and He cleanses and repeatedly prunes every branch that continues to bear fruit, to make it bear more and richer and more excellent fruit.

³ You are cleansed and pruned already, because of the word which I have given you [the teachings I have discussed with you].

⁴ Dwell in Me, and I will dwell in you. [Live in Me, and I will live in you.] Just as no branch can bear fruit of itself without abiding in (being vitally united to) the vine, neither can you bear fruit unless you abide in Me.

⁵ I am the Vine; you are the branches. Whoever lives in Me and I in him bears much (abundant) fruit. However, apart from Me [cut off from vital union with Me] you can do nothing.

⁶ If a person does not dwell in Me, he is thrown out like a [broken-off] branch, and withers; such branches are gathered up and thrown into the fire, and they are burned. (John 15:1-6 AMP)

As a man, Jesus said He could do only that which He saw the Father doing.

Jesus gave them this answer: "Very truly I tell you, the Son can do nothing by himself; he can do only what he sees his Father doing, because whatever the Father does the Son also does. (John 5:19 NIV)

I am able to do nothing from Myself [independently, of My own accord— but only as I am taught by God and as I get His orders]. Even as I hear, I judge [I decide as I am bidden to decide. As the voice comes to Me, so I give a decision], and My judgment is right (just, righteous), because I do not seek or consult My own will [I have no desire to do what is pleasing to Myself, My own aim, My own purpose] but only the will and pleasure of the Father Who sent Me.
(John 5:30 AMP)

Clearly, as a man, Jesus was as dependent on the Father as we are dependent on Him. As branches we must stay attached to the vine (Jesus). Simply, we do that by abiding in Him through faith and keeping His commandments (His law).

And whatever we ask we receive from Him, because we keep His commandments and do those things that are pleasing in His sight. ²³ And this is His commandment: that we should believe on the name of His Son Jesus Christ and <u>love one another</u>, as He gave us[a] commandment.

⁴ Now he who keeps His commandments abides in Him, and He in him. And by this we know that He abides in us, by the Spirit whom He has given us. (1 John 3:22-24 NKJV).

It appears clear to me that when God became flesh and dwelled among us as Jesus Christ, as a man (The Son), He divested Himself of all the power contained in His divine nature and became totally dependent on accessing that power through faith in the Father. We access the same power that raised Jesus the same way He did only it comes through faith in Him being who He said He was and is.

There is no other way to find the righteousness of God except in this manner. All the religions of the world that turn down the gift of the Son and professing Christians who refuse to abide in Him by keeping His commandment to love each other will find on that day that they have missed "the Kingdom of God" that has drawn near to them. Our prayer for one another would be well to contain the essence of Paul's prayer for the Ephesians:

A Prayer for the Ephesians

For this reason I kneel before the Father, ¹⁵ from whom every family[a] in heaven and on earth derives its name. ¹⁶ I pray that out of his glorious riches he may strengthen you with power through his Spirit in your inner being, ¹⁷ <u>so that Christ may dwell in your hearts through faith</u>. And I pray that you, <u>being rooted and established in love,</u> ¹⁸ <u>may have power</u>, together with all the Lord's holy people, <u>to grasp how wide and long and high and deep is the love of Christ</u>, ¹⁹ and to know <u>this love that surpasses knowledge</u>—that *you may be filled to the measure of all the fullness of God. (Ephesians 3:14-19 NIV)*

According to Paul's prayer, when we surrender to the Spirit in our inner being (our hearts) we are empowered by Christ's strength to be "rooted and established" in His love and thereby we ourselves are filled with "all the fullness of God".

[2] Bear (endure, carry) one another's burdens and [a]troublesome moral faults, and in this way fulfill and observe perfectly the law of Christ (the Messiah) and complete [b]what is lacking [in your obedience to it]. (Gal.6:2 AMP)

Loving one another with God's (unconditional) love is the Royal law of all Scripture and our non-negotiable commandment!

If you really fulfill the royal law according to the Scripture, "You shall love your neighbor as yourself,"[a] you do well; (James 2:8 NKJV)

The Main Thing

THE HEART OF GOD

"Sir, which is the most important command in the laws of Moses?"

[37] Jesus replied, "'Love the Lord your God with all your heart, soul, and mind.' [38-39] This is the first and greatest commandment. The second most important is similar: 'Love your neighbor as much as you love yourself.' [40] All the other commandments and all the demands of the prophets stem from these two laws and are fulfilled if you obey them. Keep only these and you will find that you are obeying all the others."(Matt.22:36-40 LB)

Bear one another's burdens, and so fulfill the law of Christ.
(Galatians 6:2 NIV)

If there is a most important segment of this book I think this is it. I say that because I believe that "keeping the Main Thing the main thing" is not just a key to a better understanding of Scripture, it is the key to God's heart. Without question, "the Main Thing" is the "whole enchilada", "that's all there is and there ain't no more" kind of serious. We have earlier identified the "Main Thing" thematic as God's desire for love and relationship and how that was cut off in Adam and restored in Christ. We also have posted Scripture that clearly shows that a loving relationship with God consummated by Him, strictly according to the motives of our heart, is what He desires. If we indeed have made this connection to Him, it will be evidenced in us by the "fruit" on our tree (John 15:1-12), which is true God like love for Him and our fellow man. This is to be the ultimate goal of our spiritual lives. 2 Peter 1:2-11 lays it out as a progression of "knowing God"(vs.2, 5) "adding to our faith with moral excellence", "following knowledge with self control" and "allowing patience to develop" that leads to godliness that translates to "brotherly kindness" and ultimately, "love". In (v.11) Peter says doing these things will be our "entrance" into the Kingdom of our Lord Jesus Christ. His Kingdom is His love, His law is love and His plan of redemption was to write His love and His law in our heart as we choose to come to know and dwell (abide) in Christ. I believe that "the Main Thing" is "that secret dwelling place" of Psalm 91:1, the ultimate source from which all supernatural power is generated into the life of a true Christian. It is the unlimited spiritual bank account we can continuously make withdrawals from that will enable us to "overcome the world" (Revelation chapters 2 and 3). These statements and more are confirmed and emphasized in the following passage:

¹⁴ For this reason [seeing the greatness of <u>this plan</u> by which you are <u>built together in Christ</u>], I bow my knees before the Father of our Lord Jesus Christ,

¹⁵ For Whom every family in heaven and on earth is named [that Father from Whom all fatherhood takes its title and derives its name].

¹⁶ May He grant you out of the rich treasury of His glory to be <u>strengthened and reinforced with mighty power in the inner man by the [Holy] Spirit [Himself indwelling your innermost being and personality].</u>

¹⁷ May Christ <u>through your faith [actually] dwell</u> (settle down, <u>abide,</u> make His permanent home) <u>in your hearts! May you be rooted deep in love and founded securely on love,</u>

¹⁸ That you may have <u>the power</u> and be strong to apprehend and grasp with all the saints [God's devoted people, the experience of that love] what is the breadth and length and height and depth [of it];

[19] [That you may really <u>come] to know</u> [practically, [b]through <u>experience for yourselves] the love of Christ,</u> which far surpasses [c]mere knowledge [without experience]; that you may be filled [through all your being] [d]unto all the fullness of God [<u>may have the richest measure of the divine Presence,</u> and [e]<u>become a body wholly filled and flooded with God Himself]!</u> (Ephesians 3:14-19 AMP)

I hope you read through that passage slowly and allowed your heart to focus on what is being said. The part I most want all of us to get is this: "When Christ is allowed to make His permanent home in our hearts through our faith, we will be rooted deeply and founded securely on love, which is the power to experience God-like love (the power source itself) and by the experience of His love, we far exceed merely knowing about God and are actually filled with His divine presence (the very essence of God Himself). I am convinced that every human being is created with the need for this kind of love but it is not possible for us to love like he does (and requires of us) unless we are connected through Him by that very love.

[4] Remain in me, as I also remain in you. No branch can bear fruit by itself; it must remain in the vine. <u>Neither can you bear fruit unless you remain in me.</u>

"I am the vine; you are the branches. If you remain in me and I in you, you will bear much fruit; <u>apart from me you can do nothing.</u> [6] If you do not remain in me, you are like a branch that is thrown away and withers; such branches are picked up, thrown into the fire and burned. [7] If you remain in me and my words remain in you, ask whatever you wish, and it will be done for you. (John 15:4-7 NIV)

When we are united with Him in love (the secret dwelling place) we have tapped into every thing heaven has to offer (both now and for eternity):

How we praise God, the Father of our Lord Jesus Christ, who has blessed
us with every blessing in heaven because we belong to Christ. Long ago, even
before he made the world, God chose us to be his very own through what
Christ would do for us; he decided then to make us holy in his eyes, without a
single fault—we who stand before him covered with his love.
(Ephesians 1:3-4 TLB)

Jesus Christ and the love He consists of is surely "the Main Thing". I believe that we humans are created with an inbuilt receptacle (a primary component requirement of our makeup) that can only be filled with His kind of love. When we don't have it (our choice) we malfunction. The life that people are yearning for (without knowing) can only be found in this love He offers. It is this "love compartment" that people are trying to fill with all manner of substitutes, ("Looking for love in all the wrong places"). Alcohol, drugs, sex, political and social power, the American dream are all examples of types of phony replacement deceptions men pursue attempting to pacify that basic need to love and be loved. Jesus said in John 10:10 : " I have come that they might have life and that they may have it more abundantly". According to Vines Expository Dictionary, the word for life in the Greek is *zoe*. It means "life as God has it, that which the Father has in Himself, and which He gave to the Incarnate Son to have in Himself". 1

"The way, the truth and the life" is love; loving God and each other with the love that we can only get from Him

I believe that everything in life is an "empty pursuit" without the love of God. A life without God is an unfulfilled life at best. At the worst, an unloved and unloving person can turn into an evil monster. To me, that explains why the forces of darkness focus so heavily on the breakdown of the family (God's prototype for love and caring).

I would think it would be obvious to all that the world today is "sinking deeper into degradation and moral decay" everyday and has become a more dangerous, evil place to be. I believe that all that is wrong in the world can be identified in its hostility toward "the Main Thing" (God Who IS love). Consider how much of the wickedness and terroristic activity so prevalent today is based in man's hatred of one another. We have seen that the entire universe is held together by the "Word of His power"(His power is love). It makes sense that creation would be coming apart without His love. People are hurting each other because they are so wounded themselves. Lives are being wasted (perishing) because people love themselves above all and refuse to love others. This truth was prophesied long ago. Another unpopular realization from Scripture:

> *Remember this! In the last days there will be many troubles, ² because people will love themselves, love money, brag, and be proud. They will say evil things against others and will not obey their parents or be thankful or be the kind of people God wants. ³ They will not love others, will refuse to forgive, will gossip, and will not control themselves. They will be cruel, will hate what is good, ⁴ will turn against their friends, and will do foolish things without thinking. They will be conceited, will love pleasure instead of God, ⁵ and will act as if they serve God but will not have his power. Stay away from those people. (2 Tim. 3:1-5 NCV)*

What a description of how people are acting today. If one is unsure if we are in the last days or not, this should serve as compelling evidence. Let's walk through what was just said. There will be many troubles (perilous times in some translations) BECAUSE people "love themselves and will not love others". Now please notice that Scripture says these inhabitants "will act as if they are serving God but will not have His power". Do you think this is referring to just non- Christian people? Maybe so, but I think Paul was speaking of "acting as if they serve our God". If otherwise, I believe he would have said "other gods" and would not have suggested that any other God would have (His power). I also think the reference to not having His power is linked to their refusal to love others more than themselves.

Of all people on earth, we Christians are supposed to be the "salt of the earth", modeling the mirror opposite of selfishness to the lost and dying world through our "love" for one another. So how well are we doing? I think we by divine mandate are expected to be doing a much better job in this regard than we are presently achieving.

I think we have to regroup and take stark examination of our walk with God. Are we being deceived into supposing we are obeying "the command to love like He does" because we go to church and/or involve ourselves in "Christian" duties and activities?

How many times has Jesus tried to tell us that it is not those who <u>profess</u> to be His but those who are actually **<u>doing</u>** what He commanded us to do and what He modeled for us while He was here on earth? Here is but one of those passages:

> *"A new command I give you: Love one another. As I have loved you, so you <u>must</u> love one another. ³⁵ <u>By this everyone will know that you are my disciples,</u> if you love one another."(John 13:34-35 NIV)*

Please note that Jesus said we <u>MUST</u> love one another. That sure sounds non negotiable to me.

> *When I am raised to life again, you will know that I am in my Father, and you are in me, and I am in you. ²¹<u>Those who accept my commandments and obey them</u> are the ones who love me. And because they love me, my Father will love them. And I will love them and reveal myself to each of them." (John 14:20-21 NLB)*

Not everyone who says Lord, Lord but he who does the will of My Father in heaven.

> *We know that we have come to know him <u>if we keep his commands</u>. Whoever says, "I know him," but <u>does not do what he commands is a liar</u>, and the truth is not in that person. (1John 2:3-4 NIV)*

THE HEART OF GOD

Professing to be Christian but not loving each other is **lying.**

Christian brothers and sisters, this is serious stuff. We <u>must</u> get back to "the Main Thing", the fundamental foundation of our faith, walking in love toward one another as we have been commanded.

God is love (1 John 4:8). We are created in His image. We are commanded to appropriate His love and walk in it. This is the order our life will reflect if we have really chosen Him. This isn't just page filler for sermons. The kind of love that God is describing in the commands is defined like this in [2]Vines Expository Dictionary. I quote:

- *"to express the essential nature of God"*
- *"an exercise of the divine will in deliberate choice, made without assignable cause, save that which lies in the very nature of God Himself"*
- *"love had its perfect expression among men in the Lord Jesus Christ, Christian love is the fruit of His Spirit in the Christian"*
- *"it is an unselfish love, ready to serve"*
- *"Christian love, whether exercised toward the brethren, or toward men generally is not an impulse from the feelings, it does not always run with the natural inclinations, nor does it spend itself only upon those for whom some affinity is discovered. Love seeks the welfare of all (Rom. 15:2) and works no ill to any (13:8-10). 2*

The Apostle Paul describes love to the Corinthian church like this; remembering God IS love, try reading by exchanging "God" for the word "love":

<u>(God)</u> Love is patient and kind. <u>(God)</u> Love is not jealous, it <u>(God)</u> does not brag, and it <u>(God)</u> is not proud. <u>(God)</u> Love is not rude, <u>(God)</u> is not selfish, and <u>(God)</u> does not get upset with others. <u>(God)</u> Love does not count up wrongs that have been done. <u>(God)</u> Love takes no pleasure in evil but rejoices over the truth. <u>(God)</u> Love patiently accepts all things. It <u>(God)</u> always trusts, always hopes, and always endures. <u>(God)</u> Love never ends (1 Cor. 13:4-8 NCV)

Can you see why I say that the very heart of God is love and concern for others? One might be surprised if he went back over the Old Testament and focused on how many times the heart of God is on display. Time and again the Word is clear about how important it is to God that His people take care of the poor, helpless and needy in our midst. He is equally clear about His displeasure with those who would not pay heed to "His heart". Were you aware that this unconcern for God's heart was one of the reasons He destroyed Sodom:

> *Now this was the sin of your sister Sodom: She and her daughters were arrogant, overfed and unconcerned; <u>they did not help the poor and needy.</u>*
> *(Ezekiel 16:49 NIV)*

One more example of God's true heart from the Old Testament and then we will move on. In the 58th chapter of Isaiah, the house of Jacob had filed a complaint that they were doing what they thought was the will of God and He would take no notice or acknowledge their "good deeds". They protested that they were "seeking God daily", "delighting to know His ways", were doing "righteousness as a nation", "had not forsaken the ordinances of justice", "and took delight in approaching God". Wow. That sounds like they were ready for sainthood, wouldn't you agree. Look what God told them about why they were missing the mark, the "main thing" of His heart:

> *No, the kind of fast I want is that you stop oppressing those who work for you and treat them fairly and give them what they earn. I want you to <u>share your food with the hungry</u> and bring right into your own homes <u>those who are helpless, poor, and destitute. Clothe those who are cold, and don't hide from relatives who need your help.</u>*

> *<u>If you do</u> these things, God will shed his own glorious light upon you. He will <u>heal you;</u> your godliness will lead you forward, goodness will be a shield before you, and the glory of the Lord will protect you from behind.' Then, <u>when you call, the Lord will answer.</u> "Yes, I am here," he will quickly reply. All you need to do is to <u>stop oppressing the weak</u> and stop making false accusations and spreading vicious rumors! (Isaiah 58:6-9 TLB)*

Here again we see how far religion (manmade ideas of what God wants) is away from the heart of God. He does not want dutiful service. He wants our hearts to be like His. He <u>requires</u> that we "love our neighbor as much as we love ourselves".

If you are still not convinced regarding the commandments of Jesus, read 1 John over a couple of times. (Notice how many times "abiding" in Christ is mentioned). Then go see what "abide" means. Take note of how many times loving one another comes up. In chapter 3 verse 10, it very clearly says that he who does not love his brother is not of God. In verse 14 it is explicit how the test of whether we have eternal life or not is based on the "commandment" Jesus was referring to: "loving the brethren". Then you might go through Paul's letters and see how many times he makes reference to "the commandment".

Why is it so important that we get this? Religion is far too prevalent in the church today. Religion is not reaching the lost. Religion drives people away. Jesus' disciples, walking with Him by obeying His commandments, abiding in His love and actually demonstrating that love to people around them is the irresistible force that draws people to Him.

I heard the story from a pastor of a large church in the Midwest of a woman who came to one of his services as her last day before taking her own life out of desperation. She told this pastor that she changed her mind, not because of anything he preached that day, but because of the warm, loving smile and brief interaction she got from a lady whose car was parked next to hers as they were leaving the service. That simple conveyance of love by a real Christian saved a life.

I recently heard another about a very famous athlete that will remain nameless because I have been unable to confirm the story. He said "I didn't need people telling me I was a drunk and a womanizer. I already knew that. What I needed was the person that told me in such a caring, compassionate way that Jesus loved me anyway and he could do something about my condition if I would let Him".

At a large men's gathering not long ago, I was impressed by the love of God I sensed coming off of this huge, tough appearing man who was invited to share the true Gospel of Christ with his music. During one of the praise segments this man testified that he had been in prison, was a rogue biker, an alcoholic and drug addict. He said all that changed one night as he was leaving a bar and was approached by this older, grandmother aged woman who witnessed to Him about the love of Christ. He said I have no idea what she said to me. All I know was there was so much love and caring for me in her exchange with me that it changed my life. Now he is impacting the world advancing the Kingdom of God through his music and testimony of love.

Okay, there is much, much more of this but enough already. Let's get back to why this is the most important "main thing".

All right, here goes. I repeat that I think the majority of professing Christians need to be much more focused on the "Main Thing". Why is that? Loving like God requires does not come easy and I think it is common to believe we are walking in love because we confess to know Jesus, go to church and occasionally do something good for some one. Unconditional love does not come natural and takes special effort and commitment on our part. I call it a "quality decision" and will have more to say about that later. This is not popular but they are the words of Jesus. He says that the majority of people will not be willing to accept the sacrifice to love others the way He prescribes for us to find the (zoe) life.

The Golden Rule

[12] *"Do to others whatever you would like them to do to you. This is the essence of all that is taught in the law and the prophets. (Matt.7:12 NLT)*

The Narrow Gate

[13] "You can enter God's Kingdom only through the narrow gate. The highway to hell [a] is broad, and its gate is wide for the many who choose that way. [14] But the gateway to life is very narrow and the road is <u>difficult</u>, and <u>only a few ever find it</u>. (Matt.7:13-14 NLT)

Please don't overlook that the beginning of this passage refers to "the main thing" the commandment to love God and our neighbor that "all the Law and the Prophets hangs on".

I hope I have been successful in communicating that "the Main Thing" is God's heart and God's heart is unconditional love.

Man was created in the image of God, correct?

[7] So God created man <u>in His own image, in the image and likeness of God</u> He created him; male and female He created them. (Gen.1:27 AMP)

I believe that means that we were formed to be like our Father to love like He does. It makes a lot of sense to me that man was made with a heart to love like God loves. After the fall, our hearts were changed to "know evil". Evil focuses on self-love rather than God's love. This heart change caused a separation from our Creator that was the intent of the devil in the garden. The fall changed our hearts to love ourselves more than God and others. God calls that sin. This heart change was not physical but spiritual. Repairing our heart damage and reversing the "evil" that was the result would have to be spiritual as well.

But this is the <u>new covenant</u> I will make with the people of Israel on that day, [a] says the Lord: I will put my laws in their minds, and <u>I will write them on their hearts</u>. I will be their God, and they will be my people. (Heb. 8:10 NLT)

The only spiritual heart transplant surgeon available to expedite this process within the legal bounds of God's just nature was Jesus Christ (God in the flesh). Jesus said after His death and resurrection, the Holy Spirit would come to facilitate the transfer from "evil" heart to "a heart like God's. What is "the law that He writes back on our hearts"? Isn't it to love Him with all our heart, soul and mind and to love others at least as much as we love ourselves? Remember, Jesus said if we follow those two rules we perfectly fulfill the requirements of a Holy and just God, obtain release from the kingdom of darkness and are transported back into His Kingdom (God's love).

> *He has delivered us from the power of darkness and conveyed us into the kingdom of the <u>Son of His love,</u> [14] in whom we have redemption through His blood, [a] the forgiveness of sins.(Col.1:13 NKJV)*

A wise person I know said that it doesn't really do much good to bring awareness of a problem unless you also provide solutions. In the "How I Got Here" chapter I will be sharing what I believe we can do to access the love of God in Christ and how to find that "secret dwelling place" that leads us through the "narrow gate" to the life God paid such a tremendous price for us to have.

Surely the very heart of God is "Zoe" life—His unconditional love!!

WHAT DOES GOD WANT FROM ME

From what I can gather from published data, over 90% of Americans say they believe in some form of god. I saw where a Cambridge University survey stated that approximately 88% of people in the world believe in a "higher power", an unseen influence greater than themselves. Students know that throughout history man has sought to "worship" some form of deity in their respective cultures. Ancient Roman and Greek gods, Egyptian pagan deities, sun gods, moon gods, love gods, war gods and on and on. Few if any culture has ever existed that did not have an object of worship? Why does man seem to have this innate need to revere or respect something larger than his earthly life consciousness? The Bible has the answer:

> *But God shows his anger from heaven against all sinful, evil men who push away the truth from them.* [19] *For the <u>truth about God is known to them instinctively.</u>[a] <u>God has put this knowledge in their hearts.</u> [20] Since earliest times men have seen the earth and sky and all God made, and have known of his existence and great eternal power. So they will have no excuse when they stand before God at Judgment Day. (Romans 1:18-20 TLB)*

There it is plain and simple. The One True God, our Creator, the Living God has put it in our hearts to know intuitively that there is "a great eternal power" that exists. We are expected to have sense enough to know that all of creation around us did not make itself or just come into being without a first cause or "an intelligent designer". An intelligent being would also surely be a "purposeful" one. There must be a point behind the creation of mankind. I believe the Bible tells us plainly the rationale behind why God created man and what He wants from human kind. He has made it a component of our makeup to seek after something greater than ourselves and He wants it to be Him! **He wants our heart!**

I have never seen better insight into this aspect of God pursuing our hearts than can be found in the writing and teaching of John Eldredge. His Ransomed Heart ministry focuses on revealing from Scripture information God is allowing us to understand with regard to His heart toward us and what He is looking for "in our hearts toward Him". I highly recommend John's material for insight into the war that is constantly raging for the hearts of men between God and "that ancient serpent called the devil". The Bible is all God's story but satan is allowed for a while to have a part in the play. Love gives us a choice. If we decide that we would rather have "the serpent" than Him, God lets us have our "own way". Still, the very essence of His character is love. The "Main Thing" is all about His love. **Life is God's love story!**

One example highly relevant to this concept can be seen in this excerpt from Eldredge's book *The Sacred Romance*:

"Suppose there was a king who loved a humble maiden. The king was like no other king. No one dared breathe a word against him, for he had the strength to crush all opponents. And yet this mighty king was melted by love for a humble maiden. How could he declare his love for her? In an odd sort of way, his kingliness tied his hands. If he brought her to the palace and crowned her head with jewels and clothed her body in royal robes, she would surely not resist-no one dared resist him. But would she love him?

She would say she loved him, of course, but would she truly? Or would she live with him in fear, nursing a private grief for the life she had left behind? Would she be happy at his side? How could he know? If he rode to her forest cottage in his royal carriage, with an armed escort waving bright banners, that too would overwhelm her. He did not want a cringing subject. He wanted a lover, an equal. He wanted her to forget that he was a king and she a humble maiden and to let shared love cross the gulf between them. For it is only in love that the unequal can be made equal. (as quoted in Disappointment with God)

The king clothes himself as a beggar and renounces his throne in order to win her hand. The Incarnation, the life and the death of Jesus, answers once and for all the question, "What is God's heart toward me?" This is why Paul says in Romans 5, "Look here, at the Cross. Here is the demonstration of God's heart. At the point of our deepest betrayal, when we had run our farthest from him and gotten so lost in the woods we could never find our way home, God came and died to rescue us." 1

The following is an over simplification but descriptive of my understanding. God created man in an offering of love. He put it in our hearts to need someone other than just ourselves and He wanted it to be Him. His overall plan required that we have a choice to accept and reciprocate His love or reject it.

Satan, that adversary spirit we talked of in a previous segment, because he desired to be "the main thing" (like the Most High God--- Isaiah 14:12-14), interferes with God's plan through deception by exploiting man's free will to choose and seeking to arrest men's hearts away from the loving God. Man is duped into unwittingly choosing satan over God through disobedience. Man's intuitive heart to trust totally in His God is now changed to "seek after its own" instead of God's love. (See what "love" is not in 1 Cor. 13:5).

God quickly responds with another example of His character, His grace (an expression of His love) extended to this man He created who now is an undeserving recipient. Beginning in Genesis 3:15 and all the way through the Bible, we experience God's unexplainable love as the "Main Thing" is prophesied to Abraham, Moses and all the prophets and reaches its height of expression throughout the New Testament . God puts forth the "promise" that He Himself is coming to earth, taking the form of a human (Jesus Christ) for the purpose of reversing the damage done by satan and giving us a second chance to use our free will to "rejoin" Him in His love story.

All of this activity is spiritual and takes place in the "heart" (the innermost part) of man. It was actually this "core location" within man that was altered by what happened in the garden and ultimately countered by the death, burial and resurrection of Jesus Christ. "In Christ" is God's plan to give mankind the opportunity to receive a "new" heart that will return him to his original condition before "the fall".

> *And I will give you a new heart—I will give you new and right desires—*
> *and put a new spirit within you. I will take out your stony hearts of sin and*
> *give you new hearts of love. (Ezekiel 36:26 TLB)*

In Revelation 3:18, Jesus tells the Laodicean church that they are neither hot nor cold and that they think they are rich but in reality they are wretched, miserable, poor, blind, and naked. Then He says, "My advice to you is that you come buy from me gold refined in the fire so that you may be rich".

I think what Jesus is saying is that your stony (unloving) hearts are deceiving you into believing you have need of nothing but you are as lost as geese in a hailstorm. Repent (denounce the old stony heart) and come to Me and receive a new one.

This action is not literal (replacing the physical blood pumping organ) but spiritual and we have a choice to accept His offer or reject it. Following up His appeal in verse 20 Jesus says, "I stand at the door and knock. If anyone hears My voice and opens the door, I will come in". Real love does not push or force its way on anyone. The only way we can get a "new heart" is by first recognizing that we desperately need one (answer the knock on our door) and then receiving the offer "through faith in Christ"

The following passage from Acts sheds more light on why we were created and what God has wanted from us all along. He wants us to seek Him out so we will be able to hear the knock on our door.

> *The God Who produced and formed the world and all things in it, being*
> *Lord of heaven and earth, does not dwell in handmade shrines.*

> *Neither is He served by human hands, as though He lacked anything, for it*
> *is He Himself Who gives life and breath and all things to all [people].*

-And He made from one [common origin, one source, one blood] all nations
of men to settle on the face of the earth, having definitely determined [their]
allotted periods of time and the fixed boundaries of their habitation (their
settlements, lands, and abodes),

So that they should seek God, in the hope that they might feel after Him and
find Him, although He is not far from each one of us.

For in Him we live and move and have our being; as even some of your
[own] poets have said, For we are also His offspring. (Acts 17:24-28 AMP)

We are His children (offspring) and like most of us as parents, He loves
His kids. God pleads with us to come after Him with our "whole heart":

My son, give me your heart
and let your eyes delight in my ways, (Prov. 23:26 NIV)

He says clearly that all we have to do is let Him in the door. We answer the
knock by letting Him know that we understand we have a "stony heart".
When we acknowledge in our inner man that we are lost in our sin and
desperately in need of what He has to sell (a new heart) He comes rush-
ing to us with open arms. "Draw near to God and He will draw near to
you"(James 4:8)

You do not desire a sacrifice, or I would offer one.
You do not want a burnt offering.
The sacrifice you desire is a broken spirit.
You will not reject a broken and repentant heart, O God.(Psalm 51:16-17
NLT)

It is said that the word "heart" appears over 1000 times in the Bible. If you
are an analytical person you will find that number varies with the source
and translation. At any rate it is in there a lot and almost never refers to the
physical, blood pumping organ in the chest. Heart is used most generally in

the Bible as a reference to man's innermost being, the man himself. That which is in a man's heart is that which has its seat in that person's inward life, and that which directs the course of action that person will take. It is in the heart that decisions are made and our decisions (both good and bad) determine our ultimate destiny. **Yes, God wants our heart!**

Consider what John Eldredge says about the centrality of the heart in *The Sacred Romance:*

"For above all else, the Christian life is a love affair of the heart. It cannot be lived primarily as a set of principles or ethics. It cannot be managed with steps and programs. It cannot be lived exclusively as a moral code leading to righteousness. In response to a religious expert who asked Him what he must do to obtain real life, Jesus asked a question in return:

"What is written in the law? ......How do you read it? He answered, "Love the Lord your God with all your heart and with all your soul and with all your strength and with all your mind, and love your neighbor as yourself". "You have answered correctly", Jesus replied. "Do this and you will live" (Luke 10:26-28).

The truth of the Gospel is intended to free us to love God and others with our whole heart. When we ignore this heart aspect of our faith and try to live out our religion solely as correct doctrine or ethics, our passion is crippled, or perverted, and the divorce of our soul from the heart purposes of God toward us is deepened. The religious technocrats of Jesus' day confronted Him with what they believed were the standards of a life pleasing to God. The external life, they argued, the life of ought and duty and service was what mattered. "You're dead wrong," Jesus said. "In fact, you're just plain dead (whitewashed tombs). What God cares about is the inner life, the life of the heart" (Matt. 23:25-28). Throughout the Old and New Testaments, the life of the heart is clearly God's central concern. When the people of Israel fell into a totally external life of ritual and observance, God lamented, "these people honor Me with their lips, but their hearts are far from Me" (Isa. 29:13).

Our heart is the key to the Christian life. The Apostle Paul informs us that hardness of heart is behind all the addictions and evils of the human race (Rom. 1:21-25). Oswald

Chambers writes, "It is by the heart that God is perceived (known) and not by reason.........so that is what faith is: God perceived by the heart". This is why God tells us in Proverbs 4:23, "Above all else, guard your heart, for it is the wellspring of life". He knows that to lose heart is to lose everything. Sadly, most of us watch the oil level in our car more carefully than we watch over the life of our heart." 2

Surely, it is the God of Abraham, Isaac and Jacob, Jesus Christ "the Main Thing" that created mankind for the purpose of "seeking after Him with their whole heart" in the hopes that they might find Him. Please note from the passage in Acts 17 on a previous page that "love (God) is seeking after all inhabitants (nations) on the earth" and no one group is above another. (ALL nations come from one common blood). Also see this truth supported in more depth in the "God Is No Respecter of Persons" section.

So, again I ask, "what does the living, Almighty God want from us"? He wants us to find Him and return His love. He has put it in the hearts of man to have need of something greater than himself and He wants us to choose to fill that need with Him. God IS love. Again for emphasis, the entire Bible is a love story!

1 Corinthians defines love this way:

> *Love never gives up.*
> *Love cares more for others than for self.*
> *Love doesn't want what it doesn't have.*
> *Love doesn't strut,*
> *Doesn't have a swelled head,*
> *Doesn't force itself on others,*
> *Isn't always "me first,"*
> *Doesn't fly off the handle,*
> *Doesn't keep score of the sins of others,*
> *Doesn't revel when others grovel,*
> *Takes pleasure in the flowering of truth,*
> *Puts up with anything,*

Trusts God always,
Always looks for the best,
Never looks back,
But keeps going to the end. (1 Cor. 13:4-8 Message)

Love (God) **doesn't force itself on others**. The God kind of love is quite a bit different from the way most of us think about love. That's why God wants us to "know" Him because His love is Who He is and when we get to know Him, we will want to be like Him. God is a "heart" guy. He wants our hearts to be devoted to Him because we want Him, all for who He is, not for what He might be able and willing to do for us.

Listen to the pain in His voice as He speaks of His desire for our love through the prophet Hosea:

O Israel [a] and Judah,
what should I do with you?" asks the Lord.
"For your love vanishes like the morning mist
and disappears like dew in the sunlight.
⁵ I sent my prophets to cut you to pieces—
to slaughter you with my words,
with judgments as inescapable as light.
⁶ I want you to show love, [b]
not offer sacrifices.
I want you to know me [c]
more than I want burnt offerings.(Hosea 6:4-6 NLT)

The Bible is God's story and God's story is the big story! He has invited us to join Him in that "adventure".

He wants romance. He wants our love and affection. He forces no one but gently woes us to Himself. "The Main Thing" in His chronicle is how He loved us so much that He sent Jesus Christ (Himself) into the world to suffer unthinkable physical and emotional agony so those who choose to appreciate, receive and reciprocate His love can be with Him forever and ever.

Chances are that if you are a human being, you have at some time or other loved someone. My guess is that it is a very short list of people who have not experienced the pain of loving someone who did not return their love. If man was created with a built in need to love and be loved, it stands to reason that when love is not returned, it can cause massive disruption to our physical and emotional lives. But what about God? How is He impacted, if at all, when we refuse to return His love for us? He is not just our Creator. The Bible says He is our loving Father. It is my belief that few ever consider how God is affected when man, the crown of His creation and the object of His love and affection, chooses to chase after selfish desires without ever considering the spiritual consequences.

Time for another real story from my life that I think will help to convey my thoughts about this position with God.

Growing up, I had a wonderful father whom I loved and respected very much. When I was between my freshman and sophomore years in high school, we moved to a small town in Illinois. I was a baseball player and it was baseball season when we moved there, so I was able to make some friends faster than normal. We were not bad kids but onery to a degree and we thought we were cool because we smoked cigarettes and found ways to buy beer despite our still distant relationship to the legal drinking age. It never occurred to us that anybody was watching. Remember how brilliant you were at that age?

Well, one day my Dad sent word that he wanted to see me (in his office at home) and for me not to go anywhere until he got home. Okay, so I wasn't all that swift about the drinking but I knew when something was up here because this type action from my Dad was very uncommon. I knew this was probably not going to be good and I was not looking forward to the encounter. Thoughts were racing through my mind concerning "what is this about".

When Dad finally got home, we went into the office and he shut the door behind him. Now I know for sure that my worst fears are confirmed. He said to me, "Son, I've been hearing around town that you and your friends have been drinking. I have been telling people that I don't believe it. Just tell me it is not true." Ever been in this kind of a position? I wanted to lie so bad but one of the many things I had been taught by him was how important it is to always tell the truth. Negative thoughts rushed into my mind about what my punishment might be. This is really going to make him angry and who knows what the results might be. Without further deliberation and through stammering lips, I answered, "It's true". I was totally unprepared for his reaction. His countenance fell as he hung his head in sorrow and said to me as he seemed to be fighting back tears, "I would not have believed it if I hadn't heard it straight from you. I am so disappointed and this really hurts me". With that, he left the room and there was no more discussion and no penalties were ever imposed. I should have been relieved but it was the exact opposite. I was sick to my stomach for what I had done to someone that loved me and just wanted the best for me. I never once considered how my actions would affect my parents, how this would make it appear in those days like he and Mom were raising a juvenile delinquent. I never thought beyond my own selfish desire to run and have as much fun for myself as possible. I pray I am communicating here. That was the worst punishment I ever received from my father, or from any source in my life for that matter. He had complete trust in me and I let him down. His heart was "hurt" over my disobedience and thoughtless and selfish actions. I had **grieved** my father in his heart.

Just as in this true-life story of my Dad and I, we as God's children do the same thing to Him repeatedly. Sadly, I think it is rare for anyone to look at it quite like that. God doesn't have feelings and emotions, does He? He just wants me to pay for all my misdeeds, right? He is just a rigid taskmaster poised to punish me anytime I get out of line, right? He is just and righteous but those are just standards of His love. The Bible speaks over and over about the heart of God being grieved. What does it actually mean to be "grieved"?

GRIEVE, v.i. To feel pain of mind or heart; to be in pain on account of an evil; to sorrow; to mourn; deeply wounded, a shattered heart.

Most of us never give much thought to God even having a heart, do we? The Bible says He does.

The LORD observed the extent of human wickedness on the earth, and he saw that everything they thought or imagined was consistently and totally evil. 6 So the LORD was sorry he had ever made them and put them on the earth. It broke his heart.
(Gen.6:5-6 NLT)

Listen as God speaks through Ezekiel how He was impacted by the unfaithfulness of His people:

Then when they are exiled among the nations, they will remember me. They will recognize how hurt I am by their unfaithful hearts and lustful eyes that long for their idols. Then at last they will hate themselves for all their detestable sins. (Ezekiel 6:9 NLT)

The New King James Version translates it: " I was crushed by their adulterous heart which has departed from me"

Please hear the heart of God as He laments the pain of being dismissed by His children whom He passionately loves:

When Israel was a child, I loved him,
and I called my son out of Egypt.
2 But the more I [a] called to him,
the farther he moved from me,
offering sacrifices to the images of Baal
and burning incense to idols.
3 I myself taught Israel [b] how to walk,
leading him along by the hand.
But he doesn't know or even care

that it was I who took care of him.
⁴ I led Israel along
with my ropes of kindness and love.
I lifted the yoke from his neck,
and I myself stooped to feed him.(Hosea 11:1-4 NLT)

Can you hear His broken heart as His love for His people Israel is refused?

Consider the words of Jesus that reveals the pain of rejection that God feels from an ungrateful, unloving, evil intentioned people:

O Jerusalem, Jerusalem, you who continue to kill the prophets and to stone
those who are sent to you! How often I have desired and yearned to gather
your children together [around Me], as a hen [gathers] her young under her
wings, but you would not! (Luke 13:34 AMP)

When our worship of God is based on duty, obligation and religious observance instead of intimate interaction with His Holy Spirit and His Holy Word it is just impotent lip service. What God wants from us is our heart in a daily relationship of trust and obedience.

The Lord says:"These people come near to me with their mouth
and honor me with their lips,
but their hearts are far from me.
Their worship of me
is based on merely human rules they have been taught.(Isaiah 29:13
NIV)

Another example of the same pitiful scenario:

And they come to you as people come, and they sit before you as My people,
and they hear the words you say, but they will not do them; for with their
mouths they show much love, but their hearts go after and are set on their
[idolatrous greed for] gain. (Ezekiel 33:31 AMP)

Check out what Jesus says happens when we try to worship Him on any other path than the one He himself has prepared for us to follow; **a heart connection with Him on a personal level.**

> *You hypocrites! Isaiah was right when he prophesied about you:*
> *8 "'These people honor me with their lips,*
> *but their <u>hearts are far from me.</u>*
> *<u>9 They worship me in vain;</u>*
> *their teachings are merely human rules.(Matt. 15:7-9 NIV)*

This is another time for us to inject the important message from Hebrews regarding hearing what the Son is saying. He just told us in the above verse that **any** form of worship that is motivated by any other factor than our "love connection" with Him **is in vain.** That means it is useless, worthless and an empty pursuit. 1 Corinthians 13:2 says "without this love relationship, I am nothing". The Apostle Paul says again in another place that religious customs and ceremony do not count for anything. The only thing that counts is "faith activated *and* energized *and* expressed *and* working through love" (Gal. 5:6 AMP).

The point to using so much Scripture is that I want us to hear what the Word of God is saying. The Bible is really clear when the focus stays on "the Main Thing" instead of our various doctrines and "what our church believes" and what I think based on "do I really know what".

My hopes are that it will be Scripture that challenges false belief and not the opinion of a man. When Jesus was on the earth, the Bible records that His central teaching was that He is the way to eternal life and that eternal life is knowing God and Christ (John 17:3). He said that if we receive His Spirit into our hearts we will be changed by His love. He said the way we could be assured that we have received Him is if we are attempting to live as He lived. What did He model for us (His disciples) to follow? It was servant hood toward God and fellow man. He said all the Law and the Prophets is fulfilled by "treating our fellow man the way we want to

be treated"(Matt. 7:12). He said, "A new commandment I give to you,
to love one another; as I have loved you, that you also love one another.
By this all will know that you are My disciples, if you have love for one
another" (John 13:34-35). He said when we obey the greatest commandment "to love the Lord your God with all your heart, with all your soul,
and with all your mind, and love your neighbor as much as you love yourself" we find that we are obeying all the other commandments. (Matt.
21:37-40 TLB).

The first chapter of Hebrews is all about God <u>speaking to us</u> through the
Son in the last days. Matthew 17:5 records a voice from heaven conveying the
message regarding how important it is to hear what the Son says". The second
chapter of Hebrews says we "must give more earnest heed" to the Word He
speaks or else we will be in danger of falling away (from the love of God):

*Since all this is true, we ought to <u>pay much closer attention</u> than ever to the truths that
we have heard, lest in any way we drift past [them] and slip away. (Heb. 2:1 AMP)*

**Are we paying close enough attention to what the Son is and has
been saying from the beginning?**

Is the Christian community currently demonstrating unity and brother-
hood to the world or are we divided by our feuding and fighting over
whom of us has the right doctrine? I sincerely pray, O Lord, that you are
waking us up to our failings. I pray we will start giving "more earnest
heed" to what the Son has been saying.

*And since Christ is so much superior, the Holy Spirit <u>warns us to listen
to him</u>, to be careful to hear his voice today <u>and not let our hearts become
set against him</u>, as the people of Israel did. They steeled themselves <u>against
his love</u> and complained against him in the desert while he was testing
them. ⁹But God was patient with them forty years, though they tried his
patience sorely; he kept right on doing his mighty miracles for them to
see. ¹⁰ "But," God says, "I was very angry with them, for <u>their hearts were</u>*

always looking somewhere else instead of up to me, and they never found the paths I wanted them to follow."

[11] Then God, full of this anger against them, bound himself with an oath that he would never let them come to his place of rest.

[12] Beware then of your own hearts, dear brothers, lest you find that they, too, are evil and unbelieving and are leading you away from the living God. [13] Speak to each other about these things every day while there is still time so that none of you will become hardened against God, being blinded by the glamor[a] of sin. [14] For if we are faithful to the end, trusting God just as we did when we first became Christians, we will share in all that belongs to Christ. (Heb.3:7-14 TLB)

I want to carefully review what has been clearly stated in this lengthy passage of Scripture. When the main thing focus of our spiritual life is on religious duty, trying to keep ordinances, serving church instead of "loving" God and one another, the danger is that we lose sight of the path God wants our hearts to be set upon just like the Israelites did. This message clearly says that in all their external religious practices, their hearts were actually being hardened against "The True Main Thing", God's love. If our hearts are centered in anything other than God Himself and His love, we will never find "that path God wants us to follow".

"You can enter God's Kingdom only through the narrow gate. The highway to hell[a] is broad, and its gate is wide for the many who choose that way. But the gateway to life is very narrow and the road is difficult, and only a few ever find it. (Matt.7:14-14 NLT)

The difficulty in finding the narrow gate that leads to the path God has prepared is not that much of an issue if we will consider "seeking it out from a Main Thing perspective". We must set our hearts on what "the Son is saying" and listen to what He says to do and then follow His lead. As we have seen over and over, He says we **must** love our God and our fellow man with all our heart. Going back to the Hebrews 3 passage, notice that it says, "Beware of your own hearts <u>DEAR BROTHERS</u>" and "trusting God as we did when we first became Christians". It is us, the brethren, God's people that are being warned in this passage, not just the unbelieving world in general.

I think throughout the Christian church community, it is not uncommon to see many become so heavily focused in duty and service that "the Main Thing" gets taken for granted and thus unwittingly relegated to a place in the proceedings that He cannot condone. Jesus only did as He saw the Father doing. He was able to see what the Father was doing because He made the Father's will "the main thing". He never lost sight of the Father's love and it is that love that supplies the power. When our duty and service, regardless of the form it takes, is motivated by the same love that Jesus plugged into, our ministry will be fruitful and pleasing to Him. He came to give us life but makes it clear that the "life" can only be found in our hearts finding and abiding in His heart. Religion alone will not work. I hear Him pleading with us in these last days to "please, oh please hear what the Son is saying".

All our differing viewpoints and interpretations of the doctrine of Christ are absolutely worthless if they are not leading us to that personal "heart relationship" with God that He has been so zealously seeking from us from the beginning.

It should be crystal clear what God wants from us. He wants our hearts to be stayed on Him and His love. <u>Nothing less will do!</u>

I pray that we will all examine our hearts and ask ourselves the question "Is God really first and foremost in my heart or is there <u>anything</u> else I am placing more importance on"?

Surely, it must be time to focus all our attention and effort on the "Main Thing" rather than anything or anywhere else.

My purpose and my prayer is that if you are a professing Christian, you will be in agreement.

IDOLATRY

—⊱∞∞⊰—

I believe that there is no sin covered in the Bible greater than idolatry. In this segment I want us to break down what is really going on with idolatry in regard to "Main Thing" perspective. Following the familiar format, we will look at numerous passages of Scripture that speak to how God feels about the subject. You will have noticed by now that I like to make sure we look at how a particular subject is defined first so we start off on the same page. Some of the definitions of idolatry I have found that I think are accurate are as follows:

: the worship of a physical object as a god

: immoderate attachment or devotion to something

Idolatry is extreme admiration or worship, or the worship of craven images or things other than God.

Here's a really good summation of idolatry:

"Idolatry is the universal human tendency to value something or someone in a way that hinders the <u>love</u> and <u>trust</u> we owe to God. It is an act of theft from God whereby we use some part of creation in a way that steals from honor due to God. Idolatry conflicts with our putting God alone first in our lives, in what we love and trust (see <u>Exodus 20:3-5; Deut. 5:7-9; Romans 1:21-23</u>). In idolatry we put something or someone, usually a

gift from God, in a place of value that detracts from the first place owed to God alone, the gift Giver. That thing or person is an idol." 1

I would like to submit that in the context of the thematic of the entirety of this work, the simplest and most succinct meaning of idolatry is: "allowing anything or anyone other than the genuine "Main Thing" to become "the main thing". **Idols are substitutes for God!**

Now let me say right here that I have a twinge in my heart because there is an element of this segment that sounds like the "hell fire and brimstone" messages about God I used to hear in the denomination I grew up in. You know the ones I am talking about, how God will not tolerate sin and His righteous judgments are poised to strike us down if we fail to measure up. I hate that picture of God because that is not how He is. Of course He abhors sin but maybe we don't ever really consider why. And why would idolatry be so despicable to God. Pure and simple, it is unfaithfulness to His heart intent to us, His love. **To God, idolatry is betrayal of His love!**

We have presented evidence that God is love and He created mankind in His image, to love and be loved. We have visited how His longsuffering and grace toward us is in abounding measure. But idolatry is not just sinful "missing the mark" (God's standard), it is the **betrayal** of God's love. Scripture reveals that God is way beyond serious about this subject and I think it would be wise for all of us to pay more "earnest heed" to what He says about it. God IS love but His anger and feelings about being betrayed by the man He created to return His love resonates throughout the Bible. We need to take it more seriously than we do, especially in the material culture we live in today. Simply stated, God says He WILL NOT allow any form of idol to usurp the respect that is due Him:

> *"I am the LORD. That is my name.*
> *I will not give my glory to another;*
> *I will not let idols take the praise that should be mine.*
> *(Isaiah 42:8 NCV)*

A.W. Tozer said something powerful in relation to this subject. I quote: *"Grace will save a man……..but it will not save him and his idol"! 2*

When it comes to sharing His glory with other objects or lifeless gods competing for His glory with man, God is adamant that He <u>WILL NOT</u> tolerate it in any shape or form:

Then God gave the people all these instructions[a]:

2 "I am the LORD your God, who rescued you from the land of Egypt, the place of your slavery.

3 <u>"You must not have any other god but me.</u>

4 "You must not make for yourself an idol of any kind or an image of anything in the heavens or on the earth or in the sea. 5 You must not bow down to them or worship them, for I, the Lord your God, am a jealous God <u>who will not tolerate your affection for any other gods</u>. I lay the sins of the parents upon their children; the entire family is affected—even children in the third and fourth generations of <u>those who reject me. 6 But I lavish unfailing love for a thousand generations on those [b] who love me and obey my commands.</u> (Exodus 20:1-6 NLT)

Mankind is to have no other object of worship other than God Himself. Please note how idolatry causes a negative inheritance for the offspring of the idolater who is regarded by God as one who refuses to love (rejects) Him. But look what it says about those who accept and return His love. He <u>lavishes</u> an unfailing love on them for a thousand generations (I think that means for as long as they follow that devotion to Him). Aren't we just talking about God's chosen people here?

What I hear in pretty plain language is that if you truly love Me you are My people and if you love something more than Me, you are not. As a matter of fact, if you follow after other gods, you, as an act of your own will, are forfeiting (giving up) the grace and mercy that was all yours for the taking:

> *Those who pay regard to false, useless, and worthless idols <u>forsake their own</u> <u>[Source of] mercy and loving-kindness</u>. (Jonah 2:8 AMP)*

We most certainly do worship a loving, merciful God but He will not put up with man's infidelity toward Him:

> *Therefore, tell the people of Israel, 'This is what the Sovereign LORD says: Repent and <u>turn away from your idols,</u> and stop all your detestable sins. ⁷ I, the LORD, will answer all those, both Israelites and foreigners, who reject me and set up idols in their hearts and so fall into sin, and who then come to a prophet asking for my advice. ⁸ I will turn against such people and make a terrible example of them, <u>eliminating them from among my people</u>. Then you will know that I am the LORD.   (Ezekiel 14:6-8 NLT)*

Again, this is serious business. Betrayal of God's love results in being "removed from the people of God"! To love or not to love God is a choice we make. When we choose an idol over God, it is not He who is condemning us, it is our own doing.

We have not spent much time breaking down the Kingdom of God in this work but I think all Christians would have the ultimate goal to be included in it.

The secular definition of kingdom is "the rank, authority and sovereignty exercised by a king; the authority to rule", generally referring to a corporal locality.

God's Kingdom is not natural, earthly or political. It is not a physical kingdom with a specific and limited location. It is, "the rule or reign or authority of God in the hearts and lives of <u>His people</u>". When we see the words, "Kingdom of God" we should read them as "the authority of God" or "the Lordship of God". According to John 18:36, the Lordship or authority of God is not of this world. Again for emphasis, it is "the supremacy of Christ in the hearts of men who have entered into it by the new birth".

I am including this discussion of the Kingdom here and now because God has made it understandable in His Word that idolaters <u>WILL NOT</u> gain entrance to His Kingdom:

> *Don't you realize that those who do wrong will not inherit the Kingdom of God? Don't fool yourselves. Those who indulge in sexual sin, <u>or who worship idols</u>, or commit adultery, or are male prostitutes, or practice homosexuality,[10] or are thieves, or greedy people, or drunkards, or are abusive, or cheat people—<u>none of these will inherit the Kingdom of God.</u>(1 Cor.6:9-10 NLT).*

The Apostle Paul was pretty emphatic about who will and who will not be in the Kingdom.

> *The acts of the flesh are obvious: sexual immorality, impurity and debauchery; <u>idolatry</u> and witchcraft; hatred, discord, jealousy, fits of rage, selfish ambition, dissensions, factions and envy; drunkenness, orgies, and the like. I warn you, as I did before, that those who live like this <u>will not inherit the kingdom of God.</u> (Gal.5:19-21 NIV)*

He makes the same exact thing crystal clear to the Colossians:

> *Put to death, therefore, whatever belongs to your earthly nature: sexual immorality, impurity, lust, evil desires <u>and greed, which is idolatry</u>. [6] Because of these, <u>the wrath of God</u> is coming.   (Col.3:5-6 NIV)*

Then on to the Ephesians:

> *⁵ For of this you can be sure: No immoral, impure or greedy person—such a person is an idolater—has any inheritance in the kingdom of Christ and of God.[a] ⁶ Let no one deceive you with empty words, for because of such things God's wrath comes on those who are disobedient.*
> *(Eph.5:5-6 NIV)*

At the very end of the Book in Revelation, John saw the holy city, the New Jerusalem that is inhabited by God and His people come down from heaven. Idol worshipers are NOT in residence:

> *All who are victorious will inherit all these blessings, and I will be their God, and they will be my children. "But cowards, unbelievers, the corrupt, murderers, the immoral, those who practice witchcraft, idol worshipers, and all liars—their fate is in the fiery lake of burning sulfur. This is the second death." (Rev.21:7-8 NLT)*

This exact same warning is given again within the very last six verses of the Bible:

> *"Listen! I am coming soon! I will bring my reward with me, and I will repay each one of you for what you have done. I am the Alpha and the Omega,[a] the First and the Last, the Beginning and the End.*

> *"Blessed are those who wash their robes[b] so that they will receive the right to eat the fruit from the tree of life and may go through the gates into the city. Outside the city are the evil people, those who do evil magic, who sin sexually, who murder, who worship idols, and who love lies and tell lies. (Rev.22:12-15 NCV).*

In my view, there is no need to keep "piling on" with more and more Scripture on this subject. Just know that there are many more that I could reference but surely these are adequate to communicate the message.

What may not be so apparent on the surface is how we, as Christians can unwittingly fall into this idolatry trap. God has spoken loud and clear, "I will not tolerate being second place to anything or anyone". I think He is seriously beyond serious. If we have designs on residing with God in the "New Jerusalem" for eternity, I think it is imperative that we set aside some time to evaluate whether or not there are things in our life that God classifies as "idols". I do not like to reinvent the wheel so I have found comments on a website that I believe to be a good list of modern day idols that people worship more than God:

"Life is full of distractions, desires and goals. Often, it is easy to place other things or activities ahead of our worship of God. Replacing him with another priority is idolatry. Whatever it is we choose to worship, whether it be our career, our image, or our independence is going to shape us. In Church Planter, Darrin Patrick leads his readers through a classification of idolatry, dividing it into two categories.

Surface Idols. *The more observable of the two types of idolatry, surface idols are often easily-seen offshoots of deeper, less obvious sins. Some examples include:*

- *Image idolatry- Life only has meaning / I only have worth if I look a certain way.*
- *Helping idolatry- Life only has meaning / I only have worth if people are dependent on me.*
- *Work idolatry- Life only has meaning / I only have worth if I am highly productive.*
- *Materialism idolatry- Life only has meaning / I only have worth if I have a certain level of wealth, financial freedom, and possessions.*
- *Inner Ring idolatry- Life only has meaning / I only have worth if I am part of a particular social or professional group*
- *Ideology idolatry- Life only has meaning / I only have worth if my political party or social cause is in or gaining power.*

Source Idols- *The more subversive idols are the ones that drive all the other types of idolatries in our lives. They include:*

- *Comfort idolatry- Life only has meaning / I only have worth if I experience a certain quality of life or a particular pleasure.*
- *Approval idolatry- Life only has meaning / I only have worth if I am loved and respected by _____.*
- *Control idolatry- Life only has meaning / I only have worth if I am able to get mastery in my life over a certain area.*
- *Power idolatry- Life only has meaning / I only have worth if I have power and influence over others.*

"The key to removing idols in your life is installing Christ in the center of your being," Patrick says. To escape from our idols, we must recognize them, own up to it, and turn from it. By repenting from idolatry and turning to the Gospel, we will find true joy in the Spirit." 3

Did Mr. Patrick just say that if we will keep "the Main Thing" the main thing that idols will not be an issue in our lives? That sure is what I heard.

Billy Graham offers the same solution in the following article:

> *"Well-known American evangelist Billy Graham wrote in the Chicago Tribune this week that although bowing to idols of stone or metal isn't as widespread as it was anciently, people today can find themselves worshipping the idols of money, power and possessions.*
>
> *"Take, for example, our preoccupation with money and material possessions. These aren't necessarily wrong, of course; we need them to take care of our loved ones and make our lives comfortable," Graham wrote. "But both can easily become "idols" that we slavishly follow and allow to become the most important things in our lives."*
>
> *No matter one's opinion on how these services are viewed, Graham says to put Christ first and things will work out.*
>
> *"Make sure of your commitment to Jesus Christ and seek to follow him every day," Graham writes. "Don't be swayed by the false values and goals of this world, but put Christ and his will first in everything you do." 4*

This may be just me but I don't think we could be expected to put God first in our lives over all these "things" we all need if we don't love Him and trust Him with all our heart. I don't see how we could love and trust Him without getting to know Him. Do you see how this works? Without the love of God, we only have self to look out for our interests. We then develop idols that further alienate us from Him because He feels betrayed. That's a spiritual pickle to be in.

Have you ever been betrayed by someone? How did it feel to you? In my life, I have had my love and/or trust in someone betrayed more than once. I can't think of anything more emotionally or psychologically painful than to give of oneself for another and then have that other throw you under the bus for someone or something else they deemed more important than your devotion. It hurts like nothing else I have ever experienced. That's how my earthly father felt when I betrayed his trust in me and definitely how My heavenly Father feels when I give "Main Thing" importance to anything or anybody but Him. For any of us that have ever felt the pain of being rejected or abandoned, is there any worse feeling in the world?

So what's the solution? Mr. Patrick and Mr. Graham just shared the answer with us. "Keep the Main Thing" the main thing. He loves us and wants to take care of us. Everything we need is found in Christ Jesus:

> *God will use his wonderful riches in Christ Jesus to give you*
> *everything you need.*
> *(Phil.4:19 NCV)*

I will close out this section with the foundational Scripture for my life:

> *For the pagans run after all these things, and your heavenly Father knows that you*
> *need them. But seek first his kingdom and his righteousness, and all these things will*
> *be given to you as well. (Matt.6:32-33 NIV)*

A well known Christian television personality says: "Materialism (idolatry) is attempting to use material things to fill a spiritual need". It just will not work.

MAKE NO MISTAKE ABOUT IT. HE WHO CONTINUES TO WORSHIP AN IDOL WILL NEVER LIVE WITH GOD!!!

> *Who may ascend the mountain of the LORD?*
> *Who may stand in his holy place?*
> *⁴ The one who has clean hands and a pure heart,*
> *who does not trust in an idol*
> *or swear by a false god. (Psalm 24:3-4 NIV)*

We know what God has said. Now we just have to believe it and act on it!

HOW I GOT HERE

I fully understand that there will be those who do not agree with the viewpoints I have arrived at from the sequences of Scripture presented. On the other hand, I think there will be those that agree that some or all of what has been offered makes sense. Maybe there will be readers who have not yet formed a solid foundation with God and would like to know the major contributing factors that have occurred during the progressive journey that have led me to these conclusions. It has been presented that eternal life is getting to "know God" on a personal level and that we are commanded to "love Him with all our heart and love our neighbor as ourselves" in order to fulfill the Law of Christ.

I mentioned earlier that a wise person I know said that if one is going to point out things that need to be different, one should also be ready to address how one goes about effecting changes.

I don't know if there is any one formula to getting to those places with God but I can certainly share the key decisions that I believe have made the greatest impact on my spiritual journey up to this point in my life. The following is my personal testimony of what I consider to be the most important decisions on my part that I feel have helped me draw closer to God:

1. The starting place in my case was surrender. Allow me to explain.
    I was baptized when I was 12 and a second time when I was 35. I
    went to church regularly and was even asked to serve as a dea-
    con in a large Baptist church. I also taught (very loose use of the
    term) Sunday school for a brief period. All of that time I called
    myself a Christian. There were some good times in church for
    sure but nothing remotely resembling a relationship with God.
    When I was about 45 years old, my life was not going very well
    and I cried out to God from my heart that if He was out there, I
    was ready to give up and do things His way. I made what I call
    a "quality decision" (genuine commitment at the heart level),
    one of the paltry few up to that point in my life. It was almost
    immediately that I began to experience God in a way that I had
    never known before. I am certain that God "stands outside our
    door and gently knocks until we answer and let Him in. So many
    times I have heard people say that the Bible is too hard to read
    and understand. They have no idea where to begin or what to
    focus on. That was me before "surrender". I believe with all my
    being that immediately upon submission, God comes rushing to
    us with open arms. The Holy Spirit will lead from this point and
    the Bible will start coming alive for us. He will start showing us
    "great and mighty things we did not know"

    > *'Call to me and I will answer you and tell you great and*
    > *unsearchable things you do not know.'*
    > (Jer.33:3 NIV)

    That's the way it happened for me. I have never looked back and
    I can say with conviction it is by miles and miles the best choice
    I have ever made. I am convinced from my own witness and
    from evidence I have seen in others that this is the starting point
    and we will never find the life we are seeking with God until we

make this step toward Him. Just calling oneself Christian and being involved in church activity does not constitute "surrender".

2. I think the next big move came when I got settled in my heart once and for all that the Bible is the Word of God and the final authority for all truth. There can only be two opinions about the Word of God. One, that it is in truth, God's Word to us given through spirit inspired men writing on His behalf, without one single error or fallacy of any kind. Two, it is anything other than opinion number one. Remember that "counterfeit main thing" adversary that seeks to keep us from finding God? His major weapon against us is doubt. In the garden he asked the woman, "<u>Did God really say</u>"? Then in the wilderness he tempted Jesus to doubt by saying, "<u>If you are the Son of God</u>". If he can get us to doubt the Word of truth he separates us from God. Our connection to God is through faith in His Word. Doubting and faith are antithetical (opposing and negating principles). Uncertainty about the Word of God is wavering between the two opinions and cuts us off from receiving anything from God:

If any of you is deficient in wisdom, let him ask of [a] the giving God [Who gives] to everyone liberally and ungrudgingly, without reproaching or faultfinding, and it will be given him.[6] Only it <u>must be in faith that he asks with no wavering (no hesitating, no doubting</u>). For the one who wavers (hesitates, doubts) is like the billowing surge out at sea that is blown hither and thither and tossed by the wind.

For truly, <u>let not such a person imagine that he will receive anything [he asks for] from the Lord</u>, [For being as he is] <u>a man of two minds</u> (hesitating, dubious, irresolute), [he is] unstable and unreliable and uncertain about everything [he thinks, feels, decides].(James 1:4-8 AMP)

What does the Bible have to say about the origins and authenticity of Scripture?:

[Yet] first [you must] understand this, that no prophecy of Scripture is [a matter] of any personal or private or special interpretation (loosening, solving).

²¹ For no prophecy ever originated because some man willed it [to do so—it never came by human impulse], but <u>men spoke from God who were borne along (moved and impelled) by the Holy Spirit</u>. (2 Peter 1:20-21 AMP)

¹⁵ And how from your childhood you have had a knowledge of and been acquainted with <u>the sacred Writings, which are able to instruct you and give you the understanding</u> for salvation which comes through faith in Christ Jesus [through the [a]leaning of the entire human personality on God in Christ Jesus in absolute trust and confidence in His power, wisdom, and goodness].

¹⁶ <u>Every Scripture is God-breathed (given by His inspiration)</u> and profitable for instruction, for reproof and conviction of sin, for correction of error and discipline in obedience, [and] for training in righteousness (in holy living, in conformity to God's will in thought, purpose, and action), So that the man of God may be complete and proficient, well fitted and thoroughly equipped for every good work. (2 Timothy 3:15-17 AMP).

So the Bible itself testifies that it is the Word of God. It's great if one can take that on face value and never doubt but I believe that most of us struggle in this area quite a lot. I think God has given us the okay to "come reason with Him" (Isaiah 1:18, 43:26). He desires the interaction and the opportunity to show Himself to those who are sincerely seeking after Him. Reasoning and asking questions is different than doubting and unbelief. I am confident that most unbelievers (and many professing Christians) have never bothered to examine the evidence.

There is much available in today's cyber world for "impartial seekers of the truth to find". Some of the books and other resources that helped me battle doubt with sound reasoning are as follows:

❖ Who Moved the Stone------ Frank Morrison

- A skeptic looks at the death and resurrection of Christ. This is a must read for anyone with doubts about the veracity of the Bible

❖ When Critics Ask----- Norman Geislar

- This comprehensive volume offers clear and concise answers to major Bible difficulties from Genesis to Revelation, staunchly defending the authority and inspiration of Scripture. Written in a problem/solution format, the authors cover over 800 questions which critics and doubters raise about the Bible.

❖ Evidence that Demands a Verdict------Josh McDowell.

- Mr. McDowell has written a number of books on "examining the evidence" and related topics. I have not read them all but confidently recommend his work on the basis of the ones I have read.

❖ William Lane Craig------Christian apologist (a person who offers an argument in defense of something controversial).

- William Lane Craig is an American analytic philosopher of religion, philosophical theologian, and Christian apologist. He works in the philosophy of religion, philosophy of time, and the defense of Christian theism. Mr. Craig is the most informed Christian apologist of our day in my humble opinion. His website is: reasonablefaith.org

❖ Lee Strobel-------Athiest turned Christian

- Lee Strobel was the award-winning legal editor of The Chicago Tribune and is the best-selling author of <u>The Case for Faith</u>, <u>The Case for Christ</u>, and <u>The Case for a Creator,</u> <u>a</u>ll of which have been made into documentaries by Lionsgate. With a journalism degree from the University of Missouri and a Master of Studies in Law degree from Yale, Lee wrote 3 Gold Medallion winners and the 2005 Book of the Year with Gary Poole.

3. When we get to a place where we believe the Bible is really the Word of God, we must give "earnest heed" to what it tells us to do. I have previously shared that I was a so-called Christian for over thirty years before I ever really decided to pay attention to taking God's Word seriously. If we never put into actual practice what the Bible says we should be doing, life in the enemy's world system will continue to kick our butts. Listen to the words of Jesus about the importance of putting His commandment into practice:

So why do you keep calling me 'Lord, Lord!' <u>when you don't do what I</u> <u>say?</u> [47] I will show you what it's like when someone comes to me, listens to my teaching, and then follows it. [48] It is like a person building a house who digs deep and lays the foundation on solid rock. When the floodwaters rise and break against that house, <u>it stands firm</u> because it is well built. [49] But <u>anyone who hears and doesn't obey</u>

is like a person who builds a house without a foundation.
When the floods sweep down against that house, it will collapse into a heap
of ruins."(Luke 6:46-49 NLT)

My paraphrasing of what Jesus is saying is, "what kind of a numb skull calls Me Lord but doesn't follow what I tell them they need to do and they just continue to follow after their own way"? How many of us are hearing, or have heard His Word and refused to follow yet still expected Him to rescue us from our self induced, failing lifestyle? In my mind, that is getting close to the definition of insanity (or maybe just rebellion). One more time, "He who has ears to hear, let him hear"!

4.   Next, we must be diligent about working on our relationship with Jesus. If you have stayed with me this far, you have seen from Scripture what God wants from us. He wants relationship with us. He wants a people who want Him more than they want "what the satan dominated world system has to offer" :

Do not love this world nor the things it offers you, for when you love the world, you do not have the love of the Father in you.(1 John 2:15 NLT)

If we want to call Him Lord and start building relationship with Him (getting to know Him which leads us to eternal life), we need to make a "quality decision" to put in practice what He says will lead us there. Here is a list (not all inclusive) of some of the things I recommend we do:

•   **If God is to maintain first place in our lives, we must study His Word on a regular and consistent basis**

⁶And these words which I am commanding you this day shall be [first] in your [own] minds and hearts; [then]

*⁷ You shall whet and sharpen them so as to make them
penetrate, and teach and impress them diligently upon the [minds and] hearts
of your children, and shall talk of them when you sit in your house and when
you walk by the way, and when you lie down and when you rise up.*

*⁸ And you shall bind them as a sign upon your hand, and they shall be as
frontlets (forehead bands) between your eyes.*

*⁹ And you shall write them upon the doorposts of your house and on your
gates. (Deut.6:6-9 AMP)*

- **Establish a strong and consistent prayer life**

The New Testament shows us that Jesus only did that which
He saw the Father doing and He was able to know what the
Father was doing because He was constantly in prayer. We are
told to do likewise:

*Keep awake and watch and <u>pray [constantly</u>, that you may not enter into
temptation; the spirit indeed is willing, but the flesh is weak.
(Mark 14:38 AMP)*

*<u>Never stop praying.</u> ¹⁸ <u>Be thankful</u> in all circumstances, for this is God's will
for you who belong to Christ Jesus.   (1 Thess.5:17-18 NLT)*

- **Serve other people**

*My brothers and sisters, God called you to be free, but do not use your
freedom as an excuse to do what pleases your sinful self.
<u>Serve each other with love</u>.
(Gal.5:13 NCV)*

HOW I GOT HERE

Here we are back again to the commandment "to love our neighbor as ourselves" demonstrated by our willingness to "carry one another's burdens and thus fulfill the Law of Christ. This is what He told us to do. This is what He said we would be doing if we are really His disciples. This is how He says we keep the entirety of His law. This is what Scripture says He came to show us:

> ⁴⁵ *For even the Son of Man came not to be served but <u>to serve others</u> and to give his life as a ransom for many." (Mark 10:45 NLT)*

People are selfish and don't want to acknowledge this rule. It is not that easy to do. But it is not negotiable. What I have found out, (much later in life than I would like to report), is in following this rule, we abide in Him. I have been amazed time and time again what joy happens in my soul (exactly how I cannot explain) when I deny myself and sacrifice to help someone, especially those who cannot repay. We have served food, fellowship and material necessities with the homeless and disadvantaged for several years now. I repeat myself, I don't know how but the blessing that comes from that service makes one feel almost selfish because it somehow releases the power of God into the spirit and soul like nothing else I have ever experienced. When people ask what to do for depression, I tell them to go do something good for someone else. Go serve the needs of someone else instead of keeping the constant focus on your self. Don't take my word for it, put it to the test.

This is what we were created for. To love God with all our hearts so we can "buy from Him" the love we need to sincerely care as much about the other guy as we do for ourselves.

I know it is a little lengthy but I want to end this segment with the following passage concerning how and what we are all going to be judged by when that day comes:

The Final Judgment

³¹ "But when the Son of Man[a] comes in his glory, and all the angels with him, then he will sit upon his glorious throne. ³² All the nations[b] will be gathered in his presence, and he will separate the people as a shepherd separates the sheep from the goats. ³³ He will place the sheep at his right hand and the goats at his left.

³⁴ "Then the King will say to those on his right, 'Come, you who are blessed by my Father, inherit the Kingdom prepared for you from the creation of the world. ³⁵ For I was hungry, and you fed me. I was thirsty, and you gave me a drink. I was a stranger, and you invited me into your home. ³⁶ I was naked, and you gave me clothing. I was sick, and you cared for me. I was in prison, and you visited me.'

³⁷ "Then these righteous ones will reply, 'Lord, when did we ever see you hungry and feed you? Or thirsty and give you something to drink? ³⁸ Or a stranger and show you hospitality? Or naked and give you clothing? ³⁹ When did we ever see you sick or in prison and visit you?'

⁴⁰ "And the King will say, 'I tell you the truth, when you did it to one of the least of these my brothers and sisters,[c] you were doing it to me!'

⁴¹ "Then the King will turn to those on the left and say, 'Away with you, you cursed ones, into the eternal fire prepared for the devil and his demons. [d] ⁴² For I was hungry, and you didn't feed me. I was thirsty, and you didn't give me a drink. ⁴³ I was a stranger, and you didn't invite me into your home. I was naked, and you didn't give me clothing. I was sick and in prison, and you didn't visit me.'

⁴⁴ "Then they will reply, 'Lord, when did we ever see you hungry or thirsty or a stranger or naked or sick or in prison, and not help you?'

⁴⁵ "And he will answer, 'I tell you the truth, when you refused to help the least of these my brothers and sisters, <u>you were refusing to help me.'</u>

⁴⁶ "And they will go away into <u>eternal punishment</u>, but the righteous will go into <u>eternal life</u>." (Matt. 25:31-46 NLT)

God's love is God's law that we are judged by. It really is the "Main Thing". If we refuse to love others like the Word says, Jesus says we go with the goats!!!!!!!!!!!!

My prayer is that this work I have presented will be a wakeup call for all of us who have our sights set on spending eternity with God. The sheep and the goats story is a summation of all that God has been trying to get us to see from Genesis to Revelation. He IS love. His law (that standard by which all people are judged) IS love. Our ability to love like He requires is available ONLY through abiding in Christ.

We must see that how we are judged at the end is on whether or not we obeyed the law God put forth in the beginning, not what we <u>think </u>He might require of us. Scores of professing Christians may be basing their spiritual destiny on other aspects of service (like the people in Isaiah 58 were doing) rather than what God has clearly said to us over and over in His Word. Building and pastoring churches, teaching the Scriptures, regular church attendance, feeding the poor, working miracles, casting out demons, exercising great faith, knowing the Bible inside out; on and on the list of religious pursuits goes.

The reality of it all is that we will do it His way or we will spend eternity separated from Him and His Kingdom. We must choose of our own free will to "love Him with all our heart and love our neighbor as ourselves"!

Love Is the Greatest

If I could speak all the languages of earth and of angels, <u>but didn't love others</u>, I would only be a noisy gong or a clanging cymbal. ² If I had the gift of prophecy, and if I understood all of God's secret plans and possessed all knowledge, and if I had such faith that I could move mountains, but didn't love others, <u>I would be nothing</u>. ³ If I gave everything I have to the poor and even sacrificed my body, I could boast about it;[a] but <u>if I didn't love others, I would have gained nothing.</u> (1 Cor.13:1-3 NLT)

THE HOLIEST OF ALL

—⚬⚬⚬—

The previous chapter focused on spiritual decisions (quality ones) that I believe have made the most difference in bringing about much needed change in my life and have helped me draw closer to God. There is one other episode that took place that carried so much impact in the area of getting to know Jesus better that I didn't just want to put it on the list. I wanted to separate it out because it, more than any thing else, is what has made the difference in being able to see Jesus in the light of the entire Bible and not just the New Testament. This segment is dedicated to an attempt to communicate how important I believe it is for Christians and all "impartial seekers of the truth" to connect with that resource I happened on to only a few short years ago that has made such a profound impact on my spiritual life and the "Main Thing" perspective I share throughout this work. This incomparable source is a book entitled "The Holiest of All", An Exposition on the Epistle of Hebrews. The author is Andrew Murray, a Scottish born pastor whose gems of devotional literature have made him a beloved and revered man of God around the world. This particular book was first published in 1894 and has undergone numerous editions since then.

The copy I have is an abridged publication from Kenneth Copeland Ministries. I originally purchased the book from that ministry after hearing Gloria Copeland say: "*The Holiest of All has added a wonderful dimension to my life. It has so stirred me to go on with God. It has increased my desire and determination to enter into His holy presence in a greater measure than ever before. Though this is an old book I have had for a long time, I've just discovered it. It ministered to me so much that as soon as I finished the final chapter, I began to read it again".* 1

Amazingly, after I received the book, like Gloria, it sat around for several years before I made the decision to pick it up and engage with it. It seems likely to me that the adversary spirit does not like us to connect with this information.

An Exposition means comprehensive description and explanation of an idea or theory. *The Holiest of All* does just that. It gives a comprehensive description of the entire book of Hebrews in 3-4 page chapters chronologically following the verses in the Bible. In the Preface, the author says,

"the great complaint of all who have the care of souls is the lack of whole heartedness, of steadfastness, of perseverance and progress in the Christian life. Many, of whom one cannot but hope that they are true Christians, come to a standstill, and do not advance beyond the rudiments of Christian life and practice. And many more do not even remain stationary, but turn back to a life of worldliness, of formality, of indifference. And the question is continually asked, what is the want in our religion that, in so many cases, it gives no power to stand, to advance, to press on to perfection? And what is that teaching that is needed to give that health and vigour to the Christian life that, through adverse circumstances, it may be able to hold fast the beginning firm to the end. The teaching of the Epistle is the divine answer to these questions. In every possible way, it sets before us the truth that it is only the full and perfect knowledge of what Christ is and does for us that can bring us to a full and perfect Christian life". 2

Mr. Murray also said something else that is profoundly important, *"OUR ONE NEED IS TO KNOW JESUS BETTER".* 3 That is precisely what happened to me. It not only helped me know Him better, it opened up the Scriptures to greater understanding. This happened for every member of my family that was present with us as we studied through the book together.

I have been through studies of Hebrews on more than one occasion. None, and I repeat for emphasis, none were even remotely as enlightening as this lesson. Just a few days ago I was talking with a man who told me his Bible study group had just finished a lengthy study of Hebrews. From the conversation, it was obvious that they did not capture the essence of comprehension that comes forth from this source.

According to Mr. Murray, the knowledge of Jesus in His heavenly priesthood, the heavenly sanctuary He opened for us, the new and living way by which He entered, (self sacrifice and perfect obedience), and how heaven enters us through the Holy Spirit is what makes heavenly Christians.

Without question, this exercise and experience has advanced my Christian life immensely!

The following is a little preview. Just this one chapter sheds significant light on the New Testament covenant of Christ and His relationship to Old Testament practices and procedures under the old covenant. The Epistle of Hebrews is indeed all about the "MAIN THING".

The following is not taken from the Holiest of All but straight from the Bible, New Living Translation:

Christ's Sacrifice Once for All

Hebrews 10

The old system under the law of Moses <u>was only a shadow</u>, a dim preview of the good things to come, not the good things themselves. The sacrifices under that system were repeated again and again, year after year, but they were <u>never able to provide perfect cleansing</u> for those who came to worship. If they could have provided perfect cleansing, the sacrifices would have stopped, for the worshipers would have been purified once for all time, and their feelings of guilt would have disappeared.

But instead, those sacrifices <u>actually reminded them of their sins year after year.</u> For it is not possible for the blood of bulls and goats to take away sins. That is why, when Christ came into the world, he said to God,

"You did not want animal sacrifices or sin offerings. But you have given me a body to offer.

You were not pleased with burnt offering or other offerings for sin.

Then I said, 'Look, I have come to do your will, O God—<u>as is written about me in the Scriptures.</u>'" First, Christ said, "You did not want animal sacrifices or sin offerings or burnt offerings or other offerings for sin, nor were you pleased with them" (though they are required by the law of Moses). Then he said, "Look, I have come to do your will."
<u>He cancels the first covenant in order to put the second into effect.</u> For God's will was for us <u>to be made holy</u> by the sacrifice of the body of Jesus Christ, <u>once for all time.</u>
Under the old covenant, the priest stands and ministers before the altar day after day, offering the same sacrifices again and again, which can never take away sins. But our High Priest offered himself to God as <u>a single sacrifice for sins, good for all time.</u> Then he sat down in the place of honor at God's right hand. There he waits until his enemies are humbled and made a footstool under his feet. For <u>by that one offering he forever</u> made perfect those who are being made holy.

And the Holy Spirit also testifies that this is so. For he says,

"This is the new covenant I will make with my people on that day, says the Lord:
I will put my laws in their hearts, and I will write them on their minds."

Then he says, "I will never again remember their sins and lawless deeds." And when sins have been forgiven, <u>there is no need to offer any more sacrifices.</u>

A Call to Persevere

And so, dear brothers and sisters, we can boldly enter heaven's Most Holy Place <u>because of the blood of Jesus.</u> By his death, Jesus opened a new and life-giving way through the curtain into the Most Holy Place. And since we have a great High Priest who rules over God's house, let us go right into the presence of God with sincere hearts fully trusting him. For our guilty consciences have been sprinkled with Christ's blood to make us clean, and our bodies have been washed with pure water.

Let us hold tightly without wavering to the hope we affirm, for God can be trusted to keep his promise. Let us think of ways to motivate one another to acts of love and good works. And let us not neglect our meeting together, as some people do, but encourage one another, especially now that the day of his return is drawing near.

Dear friends, if we deliberately continue sinning after we have received knowledge of the truth, there is no longer any sacrifice that will cover these sins. There is only the terrible expectation of God's judgment and the raging fire that will consume his enemies. For anyone who refused to obey the law of Moses was put to death without mercy on the testimony of two or three witnesses. Just think how much worse the punishment will be for those who have <u>trampled on the Son of God, and have treated the blood of the covenant, which made us holy, as if it were common and</u>

unholy, and have insulted and disdained the Holy Spirit who brings God's mercy to us. For we know the one who said,

> "I will take revenge. I will pay them back."
> He also said, "The Lord will judge his own people."

It is a terrible thing to fall into the hands of the living God. Think back on those early days when you first learned about Christ. Remember how you remained faithful even though it meant terrible suffering. Sometimes you were exposed to public ridicule and were beaten, and sometimes you helped others who were suffering the same things. You suffered along with those who were thrown into jail, and when all you owned was taken from you, you accepted it with joy. You knew there were better things waiting for you that will last forever.

So do not throw away this confident trust in the Lord. Remember the great reward it brings you! Patient endurance is what you need now, so that you will continue to do God's will. Then you will receive all that he has promised.

> "For in just a little while, the Coming One will come and not delay.

And my righteous ones will live by faith. But I will take no pleasure in anyone who turns away." But we are not like those who turn away from God to their own destruction. We are the faithful ones, whose souls will be saved. (Hebrews 10 NLT)

THE SON

I have determined that the most applicable ending to this work is a story I heard some time ago entitled "The Son". Chances are that if you have been around the Christian community for a while, you have already heard it as well. Regardless of the number of times I hear it, my heart stirs within me because of the supremacy of the message. I believe it is a fitting close to the "Main Thing" subject matter of this book.

As the story is told, there once was a very wealthy man who had two objects in his life that he was passionate about. The first was an only son who he adored and the second was fine art collecting. From childhood, the son traveled to the most exotic places in the world with his father as the two together sought after and added exquisite art treasures to the old man's collection. Over time, the father amassed a fortune in priceless works by some of the most famous artists in history. The walls of the family estate were adorned with paintings by Rembrandt, Monet, Picasso and Van Gogh and others of renown. As the son grew older, his love of art collecting equaled that of his father and they continued to traverse the globe together in search of the next great "find". The wife of the old man and mother of the son had passed years earlier and so the bond between the two had grown very strong by the time the younger entered his twenties.

It was at this time in his life that war broke out in Europe. Our nation was engulfed in the conflict and the young man entered into the service of his country and went to war. Like every other parent, the father spent sleepless nights waiting for any notification regarding the safety of his son. After a lengthy period of no news from the front, a telegram arrived one dark day carrying the news that the son was missing in action. Terror struck the old man's heart as he considered the possibility that he might never see his son again.

Several days after the telegram, the old man's worst fear was confirmed as he answered a knock at the front door and saw a soldier standing at attention. His entire body and senses went numb as the soldier informed him that his son had been killed in battle. His son was a medic and had been seriously injured risking his life to save a wounded man while attempting to carry him to safety. It seems the son had exposed himself to heavy enemy fire and was shot in the heart.

As the soldier left, the old man slowly closed the door and sank deeply into depression and despair, sensing the will to live quietly draining from his heart. To make things worse, it was the Christmas season and Christmas was a very special time that the man and his son had shared in addition to their mutual love of art.

On Christmas day, another knock came at the door and there was a different soldier standing on the porch. This young man had a rather large package in his hand. He explained to the old man that he was a friend of the son. He went on to say that he was severely wounded in battle and trapped with no way of escape. The son had sacrificed his life while dragging him to safety. He stated with the utmost love and respect that he would not be alive if not for the heroic actions of the son. With tears rolling down his cheeks, the old man blurted out, "So you knew my son"? "Yes" came the reply, "I knew him well".

The young man then asked the father, "May I come in for a few minutes. I have something I would like to show you". As the two began to talk, the soldier relayed how the son would frequently speak fondly of his exploits with his father as they traveled around the world together sharing their love for fine art and each other.

"I'm certainly not in the same league with the famous artists you admire but I do paint as kind of a hobby. I would like to give you a gift. I painted it myself and I wanted you to have it". As the old man unwrapped the bulky package, he discovered a portrait of the scene of the son carrying the young soldier to safety. While certainly not destined to become a universal masterpiece, the artist had somehow captured the son's physical features in striking detail along with his courageous heart in the heat of battle.

As he intently embraced the images, the old man was overwhelmed with emotion as joyous memories of life with the son flooded his consciousness. "This is the best gift anyone could ever give me", the old man said as he shared his appreciation with the soldier. "The moment my eyes beheld the beauty of my son's face and the vivid display of his bravery, this painting became the most valuable of my entire collection. I will be forever grateful for your thoughtfulness and your loyalty to my son. Thank you so very much".

After the young man left, the old man gazed for hours at the picture that now meant so much to him. He decided to hang the picture in the most prominent and visible location in his estate, over the fireplace. Millions of dollars of coveted artistry had now been pushed aside to accommodate the portrait of the son.

As time passed, more young soldiers that had known the son contacted the father to tell him of how some action by the son had impacted their lives as well. The son had truly lived a remarkable, unselfish life.

Though mortally grieved in his heart, some of the pain of loss was relieved by the realization that the son would live on through the lives of so many that he had touched.

The following spring, the old man's grief was finally over as he fell ill and passed away. The art world was abuzz with excitement when the press released the announcement that the old man's prized collection would soon be sold at auction. No one could place an exact value on the assemblage of paintings but everyone knew the total worth would run well into the multiplied millions of dollars. Museums and collectors from around the world waited in covetous anticipation for the auction day to arrive when they might realize their dreams to own some of the finest art in all the world.

Fittingly, the old man's will had stipulated that his collection was to be conveyed on Christmas day, the day he had received the greatest gift, the painting of "The Son" that had become his most prized possession.

When that time finally came, electric waves of excitement filled the air as art collectors from around the world were gathered in standing room only conditions with the full collection of famous paintings on display for their eyes to behold. All were nervous and edgy with concern over what the winning bid might be on the individual pieces they had their hearts set upon.

After a brief introduction, the auctioneer informed the "raring to go" crowd that the first painting on the block was simply entitled "The Son". After checking and rechecking their inventory directories, no one could find any mention or listing about "The Son". Looking bewildered, the crowd wondered if this was some kind of joke. Some mused that they had seen it during the review session and it was obviously the work of an amateur and would have zero appeal to anyone who knew anything about fine art. Some remarked that it was junk. What was going on here? We traveled great distances and at our own expense to bid on the masterpieces, not some unknown, worthless piece of rubbish, they grumbled among themselves.

"Who will open the bidding with $1,000 for this painting" the auctioneer barked into the microphone. The silence in the room was deafening. No one moved a muscle in response. "Okay, who will give me $500 to start us off"? Again, the same reaction, a hushed silence filled the air. "All right then, who will give me $100"? By now, the crowd was in unison with impatience. Derisive comments broke the silence above the tension as the restless crowd clamored for the first painting to be set aside and called for the auctioneer to "move on to the priceless pieces" so we can get to what we came here for.

"I'm sorry but we have to sell this picture first", the auctioneer answered back. "Now who is going to give me an opening bid"? After his request for a bid was repeated several times with no takers, an elderly gentleman stood up in the back of the room and addressed the podium. "I was the caretaker of the collector's estate and served both the father and the son for most of my life while they were living. I grew to care deeply for both of them and I would love to have the painting but I don't have very much money to give for it". "Fine", the auctioneer replied, "just bid what you can and that will get us started". The old man mumbled, "I only have fifty dollars. I bid fifty".

"I have fifty dollars. Will anyone go higher? The agitated crowd begins to calm with the expectation that they will soon be into the action but still offered not a single response. "Fifty dollars going once, going twice, sold to the elderly gentleman in the back for fifty dollars".

As the older man paid his money and collected his painting, the auctioneer stunned the crowd by announcing that the auction was over.

"What can you possibly mean, the auction is over", came the response from the disbelieving gathering.

"It's quite simple", the auctioneer retorted. "According to the last will and testament of the father,

"WHOEVER TAKES THE SON GETS IT ALL"!!!!

I recently saw a teaching manual from a course at a Christian Bible College. It was about the significance of the current day ethnic nation of Israel and the Jewish people. The manual ends with a dramatic close that states, "The key to the destiny of mankind is Israel, its people and the land".

I hold fast to the belief that the most defining event in human history is the birth of Jesus Christ. God Himself in the flesh living a perfect, sinless life among us solely for the purpose of sacrificing that life for the sins of mankind. Through His death, burial and resurrection, He opened the doors of heaven once and for all time for "whosoever will" but receive Him as Lord, "THE MAIN THING".

For me, the key to the destiny of mankind from the beginning has always been and always will be JESUS CHRIST, **THE SON!!!**

RESOURCES

The website addresses that are recommended throughout the book are offered as resources to you. These websites are not intended in any way to be or imply an endorsement nor do we vouch for their content.

Scripture quotations marked **AMP** are taken from the Amplified Bible, Copyright 1954, 1958, 1962, 1964, 1965, 1987, by The Lockman Foundation, used by permission.

Scripture quotations marked "**MSG**" are from "The Message" copyright by Eugene Peterson 1993, 1994, 1995, 1996, 2000 ,2001, 2002 used by permission of Nav Press Publishing Group. All rights reserved.

Scripture marked **NCV** is taken from the New Century Version (R) copyright 2005 by Thomas Nelson, Inc. Used by permission. All rights reserved.

Scripture quotations marked **NIV** are taken from the Holy Bible New International Version (R) Copyright 1973, 1978, 1984, 2011 by Biblica Inc. TM Used by permission of Zondervan. All rights reserved worldwide. www.zondervan.com The "NIV" and New International Versions" are trademark registered in the United States Patent and Trademark Office by Biblica, Inc. TM

Scriptures marked **NKJV** are taken from the New King James Version (R) copyright 1982 by Thomas Nelson, Inc. Used by permission. All rights reserved.

Scripture quotations marked **NLV** are taken from the New Life Version copyright 1969 and 2003. Used by permission of Barbour Publishing, Inc., Uhrichsville, Ohio 44683. All rights reserved.

BIBLIOGRAPHY BY CHAPTER

INTRODUCTION

1. Matthew Henry, *"Matthew Henry's Commentary"* Commentary on Revelation

2. GotQuestions.org a website at www.gotquestions.org, Quoted with permission 605 Stetson Hills Blvd #254 Colorado Springs, CO 80923

THE FUNDAMENTALS

1. Excerpts from pp. 26-30 (125 words) from I CAN"T ACCEPT NOT TRYING by MICHAEL JORDAN and PHOTOGRAPHS BY SANDRO MILLER. Copyright © 1994 by Rare Air, Ltd. Text © 1994 by Michael Jordan. Photographs © 1994 by Sandro Miller. Reprinted by permission of HarperCollins Publishers.

THE PROMISE OF ABRAHAM

1. Ron Jones, Quoted with permission, The Titus Institute of California, www.titusinstute.com   All rights reserved.

2. Dr. Henry M. Morris, *"Defenders Study Bible"* Thomas Nelson, Nashville, TN All rights reserved.

WHO IS THE TRUE ISRAEL OF GOD

1. GotQuestions.org   a website at www.gotquestions.org , Quoted with permission. 605 Stetson Hills Blvd #254 Colorado Springs, CO 80923

2. Rev Dan McManigal, Monergism.com Quoted with permission.

3. Justin Martyr, Alexander Roberts and James Donaldson, *"The Ante-Nicene Fathers of the Christian Church"* (Eerdman's Publishing Company, 1987) p. 200. Quoted with permission, all rights reserved.

4. John Calvin, W illiam Pringle (Translated) *"Calvin's Commentaries"*, vol. XXI, (Baker Book House, Grand Rapids, reprint ed. 1979), p. 186 Quoted with permission, all rights reserved.

5. Martin Luther, Jaroslav Pelikan *" Lectures on Galatians" 1519, in volume 27 of Luther's Works, Ed.* (Concordia Pubishing, 1964 St. Louis, MO) p. 406 Quoted with permission, all rights reserved.

6. O. Palmer Robertson, *"The Israel of God"* (P&R Publishing Co. P.O. Box 817, Phillipsburg N.J. 08865 ISBN 978-0-87552-398-9 www.prpbooks.com) Chapter 2 p. 49 Quoted with permission, all rights reserved.

7. David Holwerda, *"Jesus and Israel"* (Wm. B. Eerdman's Publishing Company, 1995) pp. 30-36 Quoted with permission, all rights reserved.

8. O. Palmer Robertson, *"The Israel of God"* (P&R Publishing Co. P.O. Box 817, Phillipsburg N.J. 08865 ISBN 978-0-87552-398-9 www.prpbooks.com) Chapter 6 pp. 167-192 Quoted with permission, all rights reserved

GOD'S ROYAL LAW

1. United Church of God, *"Did the Ten Commandments Exist Before Moses?"* 2014 Published by the United Church of God, an International Association. Quoted with permission. http://www.ucg.org/booklet/new-covenant-does-it-abolish-gods-law/gods-magnificent-series-covenants/did-ten-commandments"

THE HEART OF GOD

1. W.E. Vine, Merrill F. Unger, William White, Jr., *"Vines Complete Expository Dictionary of Old and New Testament Words"* 1984, 382 Thomas Nelson, Inc. Nashville, TN All rights reserved.

2. Ibid.

WHAT DOES GOD WANT FROM ME

1. John Eldridge and Brent Curtis, *"Scared Romance"*, 1997, Thomas Nelson, Inc in Nashville, TN, p. 80 and 81 Quoted with permission, All rights reserved.

2. Ibid. p. 8 and 9

IDOLATRY

1. Paul Moser, *"Idolatry Summation"*, http://luc.edu/faculty/pmoser/idolatry.htm Quoted with permission, all rights reserved.

2. A.W. Tozer *"Man: The Dwelling Place of God"*, Chapter 22, Quoted with permission, all Rights reserved.

3. Darrin Patrick, Adapted from Church Planter: *"The Man the Message the Mission"*, 2010, pp. 162-169. Used by permission of Crossway, a publishing ministry of Good News Publishers, Wheaton, IL 60187, www.crossway.org

4. Billy Graham, My Answer Column 2012, Quoted with permission, all rights reserved.

THE HOLIEST OF ALL

1. Gloria Copeland, Reprinted from *"The Holiest of All"* by Andrew Murray, p. 2 Used with permission from Kenneth Copeland Ministries.

2. Andrew Murray, *"Holiest of All"*, 1993, Abridged Edition published by Kenneth Copeland Ministries Fort Worth, TX through special arrangement with Baker Books a division of Baker Book House Company Grand Rapids, MI p. 7 All rights reserved.

3. Ibid. p.9

www.ingramcontent.com/pod-product-compliance
Lightning Source LLC
LaVergne TN
LVHW011227080426
835509LV00005B/351